THE HIKE ONTARIO GUIDE TO

Walks Around Toronto

THE HIKE ONTARIO GUIDE TO

Walks Around Toronto

Brad Cundiff

Additional field research by Laura Klager
Illustrations and maps by Evert Hilkers

A BOSTON MILLS PRESS BOOK

Canadian Cataloguing in Publication Data

Cundiff, Brad
  The Hike Ontario Guide to Walks Around Toronto

Includes bibliographical references.
ISBN 1-55046-100-1

1. Hiking - Ontario - Toronto Metropolitan Area - Guidebooks.
2. Trails - Ontario - Toronto Metropolitan Area - Guidebooks.
3. Toronto Metropolitan Area (Ont.) - Guidebooks. I. Hike Ontario. II. Title.

FC3097.18.C8 1994   917.13'541044   C94-930284-8
F1059.5.T683C8 1994

Copyright © 1994   Hike Ontario

First published in 1994 by
Stoddart Publishing Co. Ltd.
34 Lesmill Road
Toronto, Canada
M3B 2T6
(416) 445-3333

Second Printing March 1995

A BOSTON MILLS PRESS BOOK
The Boston Mills Press
132 Main Street
Erin, Ontario
N0B 1T0

Cover painting by Evert Hilkers
Design by Lisa Rebnord
Printed in Canada

*The publisher gratefully acknowledges the support of the Canada Council,
Ontario Ministry of Culture and Communications, Ontario Arts Council
and Ontario Publishing Centre in the development of writing and
publishing in Canada.*

ACKNOWLEDGMENTS

The writing and production of this guidebook would not have been possible without the financial support of the Ontario Heritage Foundation. Hike Ontario is grateful for their assistance.

HIKE ONTARIO'S MISSION STATEMENT

To promote walking, hiking and trail development in Ontario.

We see Ontario with a network of green trails for the public, with the landscape protected so that the walker can find beauty and harmony with nature close to home. The trails provide corridors for wildlife and recreation, linking together natural areas and spreading into all regions of the province. Through walking, Ontarians find physical and mental health and become stewards of the land.

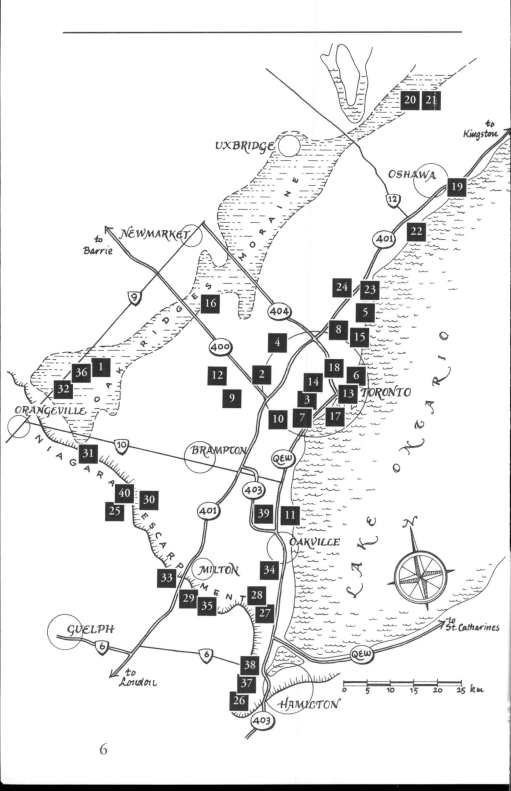

1. Albion Hills Conservation Area
2. Black Creek
3. Cedarvale Ravine and The Beltline
4. East Don River
5. East Point Park
6. Glen Stewart Ravine, The Beaches and Ashbridge's Bay Park
7. High Park
8. Highland Creek
9. Humber Arboretum
10. Humber Valley
11. Jack Darling Memorial Park and Rattray Marsh
12. Kortright Centre for Conservation
13. Leslie Street Spit
14. Rosedale Ravine
15. Scarborough Bluffs
16. Seneca College – King Campus
17. Toronto Islands
18. Wilket Creek, Taylor Creek and Warden Woods
19. Darlington Provincial Park and McLaughlin Bay Wildlife Reserve
20. Long Sault Conservation Area
21. Long Sault Conservation Area – East
22. Lynde Shores Conservation Area
23. Rouge Marshes
24. Rouge River and Little Rouge Creek
25. Bennet Heritage Trail and the Silver Creek Loop
26. Borer's Falls and Rock Chapel Sanctuary
27. Bronte Creek Provincial Park West
28. Bronte Creek Provincial Park East
29. Crawford Lake and Rattlesnake Point
30. Credit Valley Footpath
31. Forks of the Credit Provincial Park
32. Glen Haffy
33. Hilton Falls Conservation Area
34. Lower Oakville Creek
35. Mount Nemo Conservation Area
36. Palgrave Forest
37. Royal Botanical Gardens – Cootes Paradise
38. Royal Botanical Gardens – Hendrie Valley
39. Sawmill Creek
40. Terra Cotta Conservation Area

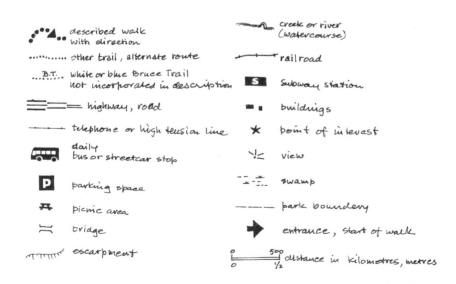

described walk with direction

other trail, alternate route

B.T. white or blue Bruce Trail not incorporated in description

highway, road

telephone or high tension line

daily bus or streetcar stop

P parking space

picnic area

bridge

escarpment

creek or river (watercourse)

railroad

S subway station

buildings

★ point of interest

view

swamp

park boundary

entrance, start of walk

distance in kilometres, metres

7

Contents

West

bluffs. looking East

looking.

FOREWORD

When our children were small we enjoyed walking the Belt-line Trail across the north of Toronto. The glimpses of nature close to home were for me an important part of living in Toronto. City people need trails and greenways near their homes; they need to see first-hand how the health of their city depends on the health of the environment. Through their experience of the rivers, hills and shoreline of Toronto's bioregion, they can better understand how everything connects to everything else.

This book provides an excellent guide to take you into the natural areas around Toronto. Toronto is fortunate in having some beautiful open spaces close at hand—the ravines, the Lake Ontario waterfront, and the hills of the Niagara Escarpment and the Oak Ridges Moraine. The trails described in this book, which are now available for walking, are only a beginning, I hope. The Waterfront Regeneration Trust is recommending a green network of trails that would follow along the waterfront and down the major river valleys. With the help of Hike Ontario and of the area trail associations—and with your help—we hope to see this network completed, improving Toronto's environment and providing many new places to walk.

I urge you all to support Toronto-area trails by becoming members of Hike Ontario. As Patron of Hike Ontario I am proud of the work it is doing, extending walking opportunities in Ontario and providing information on where to hike.

Meanwhile, let Hike Ontario's first guidebook lead you outside to explore and enjoy these special places close at hand.

The Honourable David Crombie,
Patron of Hike Ontario,
Commissioner of the Waterfront Regeneration Trust

11

INTRODUCTION

This book is about exploring where we live—not our city or municipality, but our natural region with its natural boundaries. Looking at an Ontario highway map, most people would probably be surprised to discover that the Greater Toronto Area has distinct natural boundaries. As you get out and explore this region, however, its boundaries will become clear: Lake Ontario to the south, the rugged Niagara Escarpment to the west and the more gently rolling Oak Ridges Moraine to the north and to the east, where the moraine comes down almost to the lake at its eastern end.

These are more than just convenient markers for drawing up a more ecological map of the Toronto region. As well as marking out a place, these physical features mark out a system—a system of streams and rivers that flows from headwaters on the moraine or the escarpment down to the lake. In turn, the valleys of these rivers and creeks, and the ridges and tablelands separating them, support distinct communities of plants and animals. Even within the densely urbanized core of the city of Toronto, some sense of this natural organization remains. The city's ravines and valleys can take us back to a time when rivers (rather than clogged expressways) provided the preferred corridors for travel.

The forty walks in this book rely a good deal on natural features to guide them. The walks wind through river valleys, across and around rolling hills or along the sharp limestone spine of the escarpment. They explore areas that are still surprisingly wild—such as the Rouge River Valley—and at least one place that is completely man-made—the Leslie Street Spit. The common factor in all of these places is that nature is at work.

In the Rouge, nature's work ranges from stately stands of white pine on ridge tops to the renaturalized fields abandoned by farmers washed out by Hurricane Hazel in

1954. Places like the Rouge can tell walkers a lot about the region in which we live.

On a sunny day in March, for example, we're reminded of the difference a warm southern exposure can make in a cold climate. Just as we enjoy the warmth of the sun, so do Carolinian plants that have found shelter in the Rouge. These sun-loving species, including dry-land blueberry and sycamore trees, are at their northern and eastern limits in Canada in the Rouge.

But when Toronto gets hot and muggy in July, the cool northern slopes of the Rouge may be the place to escape to. In fact, with their mix of hemlock and sugar maple, these forests look and feel a lot like the cottage country many people drive hours north to enjoy.

On the Leslie Street Spit, by contrast, what is lacking in maturity is made up for in hardiness and vitality, as plants such as aspen, poplar and one-eye daisy set down roots in what, to human eyes, looks like nothing more than inhospitable rubble. As these hardy colonizers have established themselves, they in turn have created favourable conditions for a variety of other plants. In fact, the flourishing plant life on what began as a place to dump fill from building sites all across Toronto has made the spit a prime attraction for birds—and bird-watchers. If you're lucky, an autumn walk on the spit could even coincide with the amazing annual migration of monarch butterflies stopping over on their way to Mexico.

While humans have inadvertently created a habitat for birds and butterflies on the spit, they have also, of course, played a large role in altering and destroying important habitats in other places. Walking along the lakeshore, with its turbid water and closed beaches, we see the results of destroying natural systems such as marshes at the mouths of rivers. Similarly, while walking in Toronto's ravines, we see the impact of highly invasive non-native tree species such as Norway maple, a tree that shades out competing native vegetation in all too many places.

Fortunately, there is a growing awareness of the need to restore the green spaces in our region. Projects to plant trees, shrubs and wildflowers, to clean up garbage, and to restore marshes are happening in almost every watershed. There is also a new understanding of the need to look at these green spaces as part of an interconnected whole, and to reconnect that whole with "greenways" or other natural corridors. Currently, the Metropolitan Toronto and Region Conservation Authority is drafting plans for an interconnected trail system throughout the watersheds it controls. Unfortunately, the actual on-the-ground work of building the trails will probably take some years to complete.

But even if, for now, there are no formal trails that directly connect all the major open green spaces in our region, we can at least be conscious in our travels of the importance of connections. If development on the Oak Ridges Moraine causes erosion into the headwaters of a small creek, for example, the effects may be felt all the way to Lake Ontario, the source of our drinking water. Similarly, restocking fish, such as salmon, in the lake has little effect if the streams they spawn in have been denuded of vegetative cover and therefore lack the cold, clear water the fish need.

The walks in this book will take you past a number of places where the process of ecological healing has begun. Many of the paths we follow pass through parks and ravines that are taking on a more natural look as parks departments and conservation authorities leave their lawn mowers in the garage and, instead, experiment with native grasses, shrubs and trees. Parks and open spaces are being given back their natural identities—in the case of High Park, for example, that of a savannah treed with black oaks and with an understorey of prairie plants. The difference is a park that is cooler and more pleasant to walk in in the summer and more alive and interesting in the winter—definitely a step in the right direction.

Obviously, in trying to cover a good number of walks and still come out with a book that's easy to carry, we had to make some trade-offs. We simply could not provide as extensive a write-up for each walk as we might have liked. But if you invest in a few field guides—even simplified, beginner guides—and take your time, you can learn a lot about what's happening in your neighbourhood. Keep your eyes open and stop and look around frequently. If you enjoy a particular walk, make a note on the calendar to go back and explore it again in another season; the difference can be dramatic.

Lastly, a few simple preparations will make any outing much more enjoyable. In this era of ozone depletion, a hat and sunscreen are musts. But don't count on it always staying sunny and warm; pack rain gear or a jacket, as well. Particularly in the spring when the bugs are out, it's a good idea to wear pants rather than shorts. Pants will also help protect you from thorns, prickles and burrs. A sturdy pair of shoes or lightweight hiking boots are also recommended; although none of these walks is particularly strenuous, you'll be glad you're not in running shoes when you hit that inevitable sloppy section. Pack a water bottle, a lunch or snack, this guide and any other useful maps in your knapsack and you're ready to go.

Both times and distances given for walks in this book are approximate. Times given are based on an average walking speed of 4 to 5 kilometres an hour. Always be sure to give yourself plenty of time to finish a walk, and remember that completion times can vary, depending on your walking speed, rest and interest stops, and trail and weather conditions.

Walkers following routes through provincial parks and conservation areas will often be required to pay day-use fees. For provincial parks, the 1993 day-use fee is six dollars, three dollars for seniors and the disabled. Admission fees for Metro conservation areas range from two dollars to four dollars.

Albion Hills
Conservation Area

event hikers '92

View to South West
Albion Hills, Red trail

LENGTH: Red trail, approximately 9 kilometres;
Rabbit Trail, 5.8 kilometres
TIME: Red trail, 3 hours; Rabbit Trail, 1 hour
TERRAIN: Rolling hills
DIRECTIONS: The conservation area is located 8
kilometres north of Bolton on Highway 50. There is a small
day-use fee.

Ask people in Toronto where their drinking water comes
from and most will accurately point to Lake Ontario. But ask
them where the rivers that feed the lake come from and most
will have no idea. The answer, almost without exception, is
the Oak Ridges Moraine, a long ribbon of sand and gravel

deposited by the meltwaters of two retreating glaciers millions of years ago. The headwaters of the Don, the Rouge, the Highland and a half-dozen other creeks and rivers that cut through the boundaries of the Greater Toronto Area percolate from the moraine, which stretches from east of Peterborough to the Niagara Escarpment.

The moraine is actually a large pile of sand and gravel, with the finer material on top and the coarser material settled toward the bottom. This structure makes it ideal both as a filter and a storage device for the rainwater and snowmelt that feeds this watershed's rivers and streams. However, this make-up also makes the moraine prone to erosion; strip off the vegetation and the sandy soils just blow away, a lesson that was originally learned in the 1930s and '40s when deforestation caused by clearing for farms and timber harvesting left stretches of the moraine desertlike. Since then, the problem has become urban development, which has also led to the cutting of forested areas, the destruction of of pocket wetlands, the depletion of the moraine's aquifers by municipal wells, and the pollution of the aquifers by septic systems.

In the 1940s, the solution to the problems on the moraine was reforestation, to be carried out by the newly formed conservation authorities. One of the first areas set aside was Albion Hills, in the rolling terrain of the wider western end of the moraine. This area, in fact, became the first conservation area in Ontario.

The landscape of Albion Hills continues to be dominated by pine trees, unfortunately planted mostly in endless rows. However, the rolling hills of the conservation area do make it a good place for walking in late summer and fall, when you'll be rewarded with great views across the Caledon Hills. A system of ski trails, some of which double as interpretive nature trails, has been created, and there are plenty of facilities, from picnic grounds to a swimming area.

Of the ski trails that are also officially nature trails, the longest is the Rabbit Trail. The trail starts from Albion Hills'

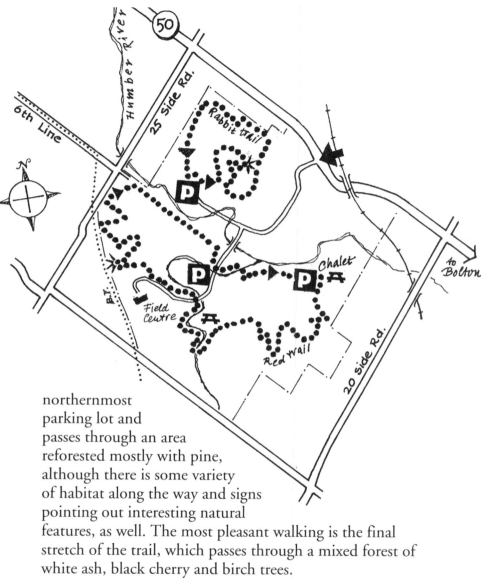

northernmost
parking lot and
passes through an area
reforested mostly with pine,
although there is some variety
of habitat along the way and signs
pointing out interesting natural
features, as well. The most pleasant walking is the final
stretch of the trail, which passes through a mixed forest of
white ash, black cherry and birch trees.

For more of a leg-stretching walk (and the reward of
an excellent viewpoint), park near the ski chalet. From
behind the chalet, pick up the red trail and follow it as it
meanders through a reforested area. At the various trail
junctions, continue to follow the red trail, which eventually

crosses Centreville Creek (a tributary of the Humber River) and then follows the creek past an outdoor education centre. The centre is

set in a pleasant meadow that, in fall, is bright with the purple and yellow flowers of asters and goldenrod. Look for pheasants and white-tailed deer in the meadow, as well. Just after the red trail once again meets the blue trail, you'll come to a spot where the red trail makes a ninety-degree turn. From this corner, there is a great view of the Caledon Hills and of the outdoor school tucked in the meadow below.

After a couple more turns, the red trail follows almost a straight line back to the chalet, passing through a well-equipped picnic area that might be a good place to stop for lunch.

Black Creek

Black Creek

E Best H.

LENGTH: 5 kilometres
TIME: 2 hours
TERRAIN: Flat, with a couple of steep descents from roadways into valleys
DIRECTIONS: The Jane 35B bus will take you right to Black Creek Pioneer Village where this walk begins. From the end of the walk, you can take the Sheppard West 84 bus back to Jane Street. By car, take Jane north from Finch until you see the signs for Black Creek Pioneer Village. Turn right on Shoreham Drive and park in the lot at the village.

The Black Creek Valley is a good example of an urban green space transformed. Through the hard work of community members, led by the Black Creek Conservation Project, the valley has been changed from sterile, groomed parkland into a more natural state of wildness, if not exactly wilderness. The path that runs from Shoreham Drive to Sheppard Avenue is paved for its entire length and is neatly bordered with mown turf. But the path along the creek itself is now lined with tall grasses, shrubs and saplings that, together with gatherings of old willows, shade the creek, stabilize its banks, and provide food and shelter for birds and small mammals. The valley may not be as physically green as it was when it was carpeted with manicured turf, but it is much more "green" in an ecological sense.

Start your walk from the visitor parking lot at Black Creek Pioneer Village by heading down the delivery vehicle access road that leads into the valley from the southwest corner of the lot. Take the first left from the road down to the valley and start walking south. Don't feel you have to stick to the paved path; there's often more interesting sights to be seen if you walk on the turf closer to the naturalized areas. Heading south, cross under the bridge carrying Shoreham Drive, and on the other side you will immediately start to see ecological restoration work in progress. On the slope to your left, a number of pioneer shrub and tree species, including poplar, ash, one or two white pine and red maple, have been planted. It looks a bit sparse now, but in a generation, this slope could become a nicely shaded spot, with the poplars in particular being supplanted by climax species such as sugar maple, white oak or beech.

Crossing a small footbridge, you'll notice two other pieces of restoration in progress: first, a dense thicket of dogwood shrubs that provides protection for birds and small animals who will, it is hoped, in turn bring wild seeds with them into the valley; and, second, a large area of what was probably turf, but has now been tilled up. This section may be planted or it may be left to seed in naturally.

The path at times draws away from the creek, so you might want to take the occasional side trail back toward the banks, being careful not to step on any of the silver maple, cedar, red oak or dogwood seedlings that have been planted amongst the tall grasses and along the stream banks.

Passing under a set of hydro transmission lines, the creek makes a tight meander that promises to one day become

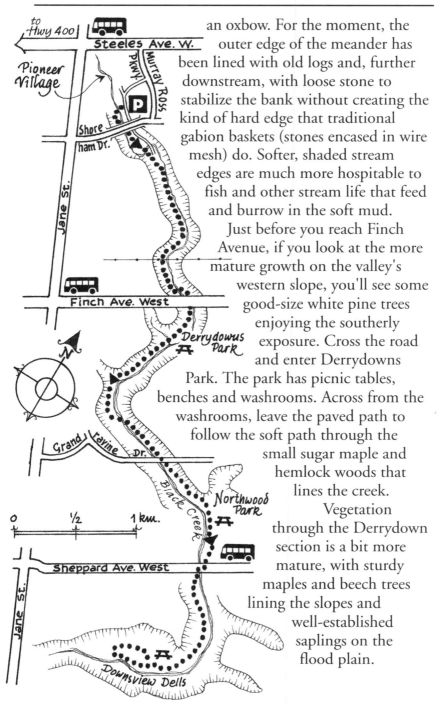

an oxbow. For the moment, the outer edge of the meander has been lined with old logs and, further downstream, with loose stone to stabilize the bank without creating the kind of hard edge that traditional gabion baskets (stones encased in wire mesh) do. Softer, shaded stream edges are much more hospitable to fish and other stream life that feed and burrow in the soft mud.

Just before you reach Finch Avenue, if you look at the more mature growth on the valley's western slope, you'll see some good-size white pine trees enjoying the southerly exposure. Cross the road and enter Derrydowns Park. The park has picnic tables, benches and washrooms. Across from the washrooms, leave the paved path to follow the soft path through the small sugar maple and hemlock woods that lines the creek. Vegetation through the Derrydown section is a bit more mature, with sturdy maples and beech trees lining the slopes and well-established saplings on the flood plain.

On the map:

to Hwy 400

Pioneer Village

Steeles Ave. W.

Murray Ross Pkwy.

P

Shoreham Dr.

Jane St.

Finch Ave. West

N

Derrydowns Park

Grand Ravine Dr.

Black Creek

Northwood Park

0   ½   1 km.

Sheppard Ave. West

Jane St.

Downsview Dells

22

Walking out toward Grandravine Drive at the south end, you'll pass through a nice stand of oaks.

Cross Grandravine Drive and head down the steep slope into Northwood Park. Here again, you'll see the hand of the restorationists at work, with sapling and seedling plantings in two or three locations. Notice how attention has been paid to ensuring that the vegetation planted not only provides shelter, but also food, especially berries. Already established crab apple and chokecherry trees, for example, have been joined by such berry bearers as dogwood and mulberry.

Facilities such as barbecues, picnic tables and washrooms are found at the south end of Northwood Park. From here, walkers can continue out to Sheppard Avenue and then make their way back to the starting point or, for those who want to stretch their legs a little more, continue south into the large picnic grounds in Downsview Dells Park before looping back up to Sheppard.

Cedarvale
Ravine and
the Beltline

LENGTH: 7 kilometres
TIME: 2 hours
TERRAIN: Flat with gravel or paved paths to follow most of the way
DIRECTIONS: The walk starts from the Rosedale subway station and ends at the Davisville station. En route, it passes both the St. Clair Avenue West and Eglinton West stations.

This route, like the Rosedale Ravine loop, offers walkers a chance to see a little nature in the very heart of the city. As well, the walk is a chance to discover some of the city's modern history, passing as it does through the stately neighbourhood of Forest Hill and along the route of the Beltline Railway, a commuter rail line built in the 1800s partly to serve this new northern suburb of the growing city to the south.

Starting from the entrance to Ramsden Park opposite the Rosedale subway station, walkers can cross through this typical city park right over to Avenue Road. Ramsden is a small park, and although it looks green, its trees no doubt

24

suffer from
the problems
of many ornamental park trees:
the compaction of the turf that
covers their roots and comes
right up to their trunks causes
suffocation and drought,
and their isolation from other
trees encourages their limbs to spread broadly,
leaving them vulnerable to breaking under heavy
snow and ice loads. Even in a park that faces heavy
recreational demands, like Ramsden, planting trees in groups
and allowing an understorey to grow up beneath them could
keep these trees alive longer.

Stay generally to the north side of the park, and
eventually you will see a gap between buildings that leads out
to Avenue Road. Walk north on Avenue and cross at the
lights. Continue north on the west side and under the railway bridge until you reach MacPherson Avenue, the first
street after the tracks. Turn left and follow MacPherson for
two long blocks to Poplar Plains Road. Turn north (right) on

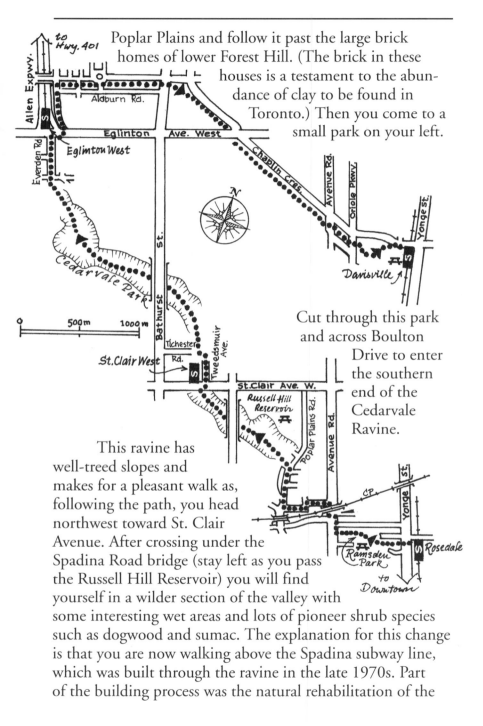

Poplar Plains and follow it past the large brick homes of lower Forest Hill. (The brick in these houses is a testament to the abundance of clay to be found in Toronto.) Then you come to a small park on your left.

Cut through this park and across Boulton Drive to enter the southern end of the Cedarvale Ravine.

This ravine has well-treed slopes and makes for a pleasant walk as, following the path, you head northwest toward St. Clair Avenue. After crossing under the Spadina Road bridge (stay left as you pass the Russell Hill Reservoir) you will find yourself in a wilder section of the valley with some interesting wet areas and lots of pioneer shrub species such as dogwood and sumac. The explanation for this change is that you are now walking above the Spadina subway line, which was built through the ravine in the late 1970s. Part of the building process was the natural rehabilitation of the valley, carried out after construction was completed. At the time, naturalists worried whether the valley would again attract the same diversity of birds it had before construction began. A decade or so later, the valley is still in an early stage of succession, but it is once again a good place to see birds. (Of course, if metropolitan planners had had their way in the 1960s, you would now be walking up the middle of the Spadina Expressway, a project that was finally brought to a halt at Eglinton Avenue in 1972.)

Just before you reach St. Clair, take the left branch of the path and continue in the valley past the lower-level subway entrance and along a narrow footpath running through some fairly dense thickets clinging to the middle of the slope. This will bring you out to St. Clair. In wetter weather, go right instead and follow the main path out to St. Clair, as the slope path could be quite slippery. Cross St. Clair in front of the Loblaws store and walk east along the north side of the street to Tweedsmuir Avenue. Go north on Tweedsmuir to Tichester Road and west on Tichester until you see another subway entrance. From the west side of the entrance, follow the path back down into Cedarvale Ravine. The ravine is wider through this section, and there are lots of marshy areas filled with rushes and cattails to explore for frogs and other amphibians. If you're there at a quiet time, birding should also be good, with lots of thorny shrubbery to provide the birds with protection from predators (of whom unbelled domestic cats are the worst) and with berries and seeds to eat, as well.

A ways after the iron elegance of the Bathurst Street bridge, walkers emerge into the open parkland of Cedarvale Park. The most enjoyable route through here might be to abandon the paved path and follow Castle Frank Brook, a tributary of the West Don, along the eastern edge of the park.

At the north end of the park are some small areas planted with spruce seedlings. Follow the path through these and out of the park to Everden Road. Where Everden reaches

Eglinton, you may have to walk west to the lights to cross. After crossing, walk back east toward the entrance to the Allen Expressway and follow the sidewalk running beside it until, just north of Aldburn Road, you see the entrance to the Beltline Trail on your right.

The Beltline was built in 1891 by a group of real-estate developers who felt a railway loop running from downtown up through the newly developed suburbs of Moore Park and Forest Hill could only add to the attractiveness of their real estate. The overambitious developers quickly went bankrupt, however, and the line was actually finished by the Grand Trunk Railway, which operated it as a passenger service for the next two years. Parts of the line survived as a freight service until the 1950s, while other parts were quickly gobbled up by development. What remains of the line has now been turned into a multipurpose rail-trail by the city of Toronto.

The line starts off running due east through a highly residential area, and there's not much more than the occasional bit of shrubbery along the trail here. After crossing Bathurst, it passes behind a series of large apartment buildings before turning to follow Chaplin Crescent (although historically, the relationship was probably vice versa). After crossing under Eglinton, the old trackway runs dead straight along a raised bed down a small ravine. This section is well treed, with oaks and maples arching over the trail. There are a few side roads and Oriole Parkway to cross, but the trail is now fixed in its direction, well marked and easy to follow. When you reach the entrance to the TTC's Davisville car yard, leave the trail (which dead-ends at the old bridge over the yards) and cut through Oriole Park on your left. Follow the path from the north side of the park out to Davisville Avenue and walk east to the Davisville subway station.

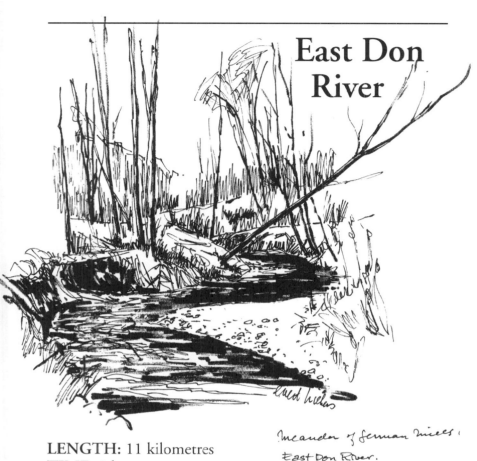

East Don River

meander of German mills,
East Don River.

LENGTH: 11 kilometres
TIME: 3 hours
TERRAIN: Flat, with some wet sections north of Finch, but paved path south of Finch to Duncan Mill Road
DIRECTIONS: Take the Steeles East 53 bus from Finch station to Steeles and Leslie. Walk south on Leslie to the bridge over the East Don. From the end point of the walk, take the York Mills 95 bus west to the York Mills station. There is no parking on Leslie, so if you drive, you will have to leave your car at a lot near the Finch station and take the bus or find parking on a side street near Steeles and Leslie.

This northerly stretch of the Don offers a chance for a good leg-stretching walk and a chance to see the river and its valley

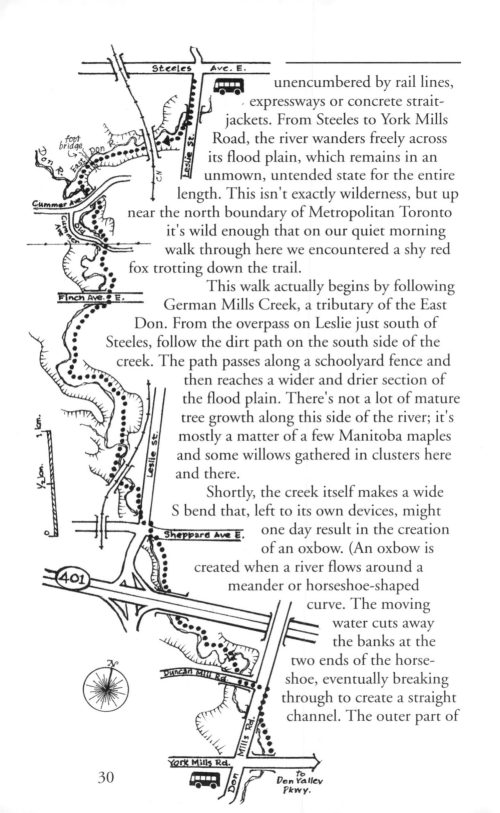

unencumbered by rail lines, expressways or concrete strait-jackets. From Steeles to York Mills Road, the river wanders freely across its flood plain, which remains in an unmown, untended state for the entire length. This isn't exactly wilderness, but up near the north boundary of Metropolitan Toronto it's wild enough that on our quiet morning walk through here we encountered a shy red fox trotting down the trail.

This walk actually begins by following German Mills Creek, a tributary of the East Don. From the overpass on Leslie just south of Steeles, follow the dirt path on the south side of the creek. The path passes along a schoolyard fence and then reaches a wider and drier section of the flood plain. There's not a lot of mature tree growth along this side of the river; it's mostly a matter of a few Manitoba maples and some willows gathered in clusters here and there.

Shortly, the creek itself makes a wide S bend that, left to its own devices, might one day result in the creation of an oxbow. (An oxbow is created when a river flows around a meander or horseshoe-shaped curve. The moving water cuts away the banks at the two ends of the horse-shoe, eventually breaking through to create a straight channel. The outer part of the curve is then cut off from the flow of the river and becomes an oxbow pond or lake.) Just past these curves, the path crosses under a railway trestle and, after this point, the opposite side of the valley becomes quite wooded.

On the path side, however, the ground is still somewhat soggy and, at a couple of points, you'll have to pass through dense thickets, watching out for thorns and whipping branches.

Among the shrubs that thrive throughout this section are black locusts, a small tree or shrub native to the South that has become naturalized in Ontario.

A few hundred metres after passing under a pedestrian bridge, the walk reaches the confluence of the creek and the East Don River. There is a footbridge across the Don at this point for anyone who would like to explore upriver a bit, but our walk continues south on the east side of the river and under Cummer Avenue.

At the point where a set of hydro lines crosses the river, the path follows the side of a steep slope to reach the abandoned bridge that used to carry Old Cummer Avenue. Climb up the bank past the bridge and continue along the flat wide valley to the south, through a small stand of maples and across a small drainage stream, before cutting away from the river and up toward Finch Avenue.

Cross Finch and follow the paved path back down into the valley on the other side. There are some large wetland areas on your left as you reenter the valley, and the width of the valley through here makes it a good place to study a variety of habitats, from slope forests to marshes to the vine-and-shrub covered banks of the river itself.

As you get further south, the path tends to move away from the river and toward the valley side. Passing a trail junction, stay right and continue in the direction of the river. The valley becomes a little more treed now, and there are some nice clusters of cedars. Just before reaching a railway trestle, the path crosses the Don on a wooden footbridge, then snakes under the trestle and recrosses the river.

Continue to follow the path as it climbs toward the top rim of the valley and then drops down again, curving around a high hill covered with red pine sentinels. As you come around the bottom of the hill, you will once again reach a trail junction, with the path to the right leading to a small picnic area on the other side of the river.

To continue the walk, stay left and follow the path out of the valley to Leslie Street. Walk south to Sheppard and cross to the southeast corner of the intersection. Head east half a block to once again pick up the path through the valley.

The valley remains quite pretty through the next section, but the proximity of Highway 401 does make it rather noisy. After you've crossed under the highway, the path parallels the 401 in an open field area that is easily the noisiest part of the walk. Fortunately, it shortly swings around behind a small hill forested with maples and hemlocks and the din decreases. If nothing else, this is a good spot to compare the serenity of the valley you've come through to the usual jangle of urban living.

Follow the path as it crosses a footbridge, turning left when you reach the opposite side. After crossing Duncan Mill Road, the west bank of the river is posted as private property, but walkers can cross it if the school that uses this area is not in session. Otherwise, follow Duncan Mill to Don Mills Road and cross to the east side of Don Mills. From here you can follow an informal path along the river to York Mills Road. In late fall or winter, you can even continue across the golf course here and keep walking as far south along the Don as you wish.

East Point Park

Bluffs
East Point Park
looking west

LENGTH: 5 kilometres
TIME: 2 hours
TERRAIN: Level, except for the descent to the beach
DIRECTIONS: On weekdays, take the Scarboro 86D bus from Kennedy station to the corner of Coronation Drive and Beechgrove Drive. Walk east and south to the end of Beechgrove. On weekends, take the 116 bus from Kennedy to Morningside Drive, just south of the CN railway tracks. Walk east along the trail on the south side of the tracks. By car, take Lawrence Avenue to Beechgrove, then Beech-grove south and east to the parking lot located just south of the tracks.

When we think of wild places, we tend to think of trees. What should you do to heal the earth? Plant a tree. But walking in the wide open meadows that make up most of East Point Park you can quickly see why such natural open spaces are also important. If your timing is right, on a sunny day's walk in September, you'll be joined by hundreds of monarch butterflies sipping nectar from the profusion of asters that grow here. At other times, you might see birds such as bobolinks, meadowlarks and savannah sparrows that prefer open meadows to woodlands.

East Point consists of 55 hectares of open, undeveloped land wedged between a water treatment plant to the west and a sewage treatment plant to the east (far enough away so that odour is not a problem). Other than a miniature grass airfield for model airplane enthusiasts in the middle of the park, there are no facilities or even formal paths of any kind. The grey-blue waters of Lake Ontario roll up on a narrow beach backed by clay bluffs, and from the top of the bluffs back to the road lies a surprisingly serene—even isolated-feeling—expanse of wildflowers, shrubs and the occasional knot of trees.

Start your walk from the parking lot at the south end of Beechgrove Drive. Head down the dirt road toward the lake from here, but follow the path to the right before you reach the lake. This path will take you to the top edge of the bluffs, which you can follow for the length of the park, and along a narrow unmown section of meadow that fronts the water treatment plant at the park's western end. Take your time and look for birds, butterflies and wildflowers. Watch the lake and the bank swallows that flit along the bluff edge. Once you reach the western edge of the meadow, you'll have to backtrack for a bit until you reach a path that leads you away from the bluff. From this path, you can swing east again and head through the centre of the park (watching out for low-flying model aircraft). This central path passes some small marshes that are good places to listen and look for frogs and toads.

The small woods and scattered apple and lilac trees in the park are the legacy of long-gone cottagers who used East Point as their city escape. It still serves that purpose well today. The park is relatively isolated and, being undeveloped, doesn't attract much of a crowd.

Once you've reached the eastern edge of the park again, turn south and pick your way down the gully at the end of the road to the beach. There's lots of driftwood, and on a warm day the beach can be an excellent lunching spot.

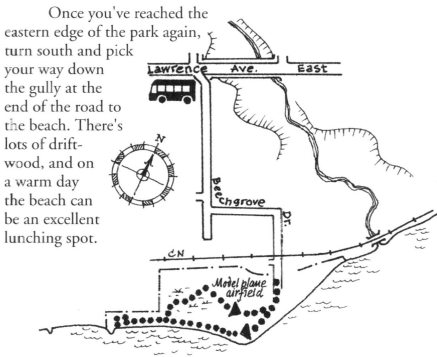

Walking along the beach, you can study the patterns of the cliff faces and watch the bank swallows entering and leaving their holes just under the top edge.

East Point is the perfect place to bring your wildflower and bird guides. The walking itself is not strenuous and the distance really depends on how much you want to wander; just keep your senses open.

Glen Stewart Ravine, the Beaches and Ashbridge's Bay Park

LENGTH: 3 kilometres
TIME: 1 hour
TERRAIN: Mostly flat. Through the ravine, the trail runs downhill.
DIRECTION: Take the 502 or 503 streetcar to Kingston Road and Beech Avenue. There is one-hour curb parking on Kingston Road.

This is a short walk but it's a good one to start with for those looking to learn about Toronto's ravine system. That's because the city of Toronto parks department has developed an interpretive nature trail through the Glen Stewart Ravine and an attractive pocket-size guidebook to go with it. The city hopes that city residents in general and school groups in particular will take advantage of these resources to learn to appreciate the beauty and hidden charms of this narrow ravine. Those behind the project also hope that growing community awareness of the ravine's natural values might help control vandalism and erosion (primarily caused by mountain biking on the slopes) in the ravine. Already, wooden number posts for the trail have had to be replaced with steel posts sunk in concrete because of vandalism. The guidebook can be obtained free from community centres and area libraries or by calling (416) 392-1111.

Another interesting aspect of this walk is the contrast between the natural setting of Glen Stewart Ravine and the artificially created Ashbridge's Bay Park. Up until the 1920s, the Ashbridge's Bay wetland was the largest and most important marsh on the Toronto waterfront. It took four million cubic yards of material to fill in the wetland to create new industrial and port lands (including the present site of the Hearn Generating Station), which now sit mostly contaminated and underused.

Enter the ravine off Beech Avenue and follow the trail along the side of this narrower offshoot of the main ravine until you reach the junction with the main path. (If you're following the nature trail guide, this walk goes in reverse order, from post 12 to post 1.) As with the main ravine, the dominant trees through this side valley are red oak, red maple, sugar maple and white ash.

You will quickly come to the junction with the main trail just below a set of wooden stairs leading up to Kingston Road. From here, a wide trail follows the small spring-fed creek through the ravine.

As much as the ravine is now being left in a "natural" state, it has plenty of "unnatural" species growing in it, from the ubiquitous and invasive Norway maple to Japanese knotweed. Still, it is a pleasant—if short—stroll through the mature forest that lines most of the valley, and it is always

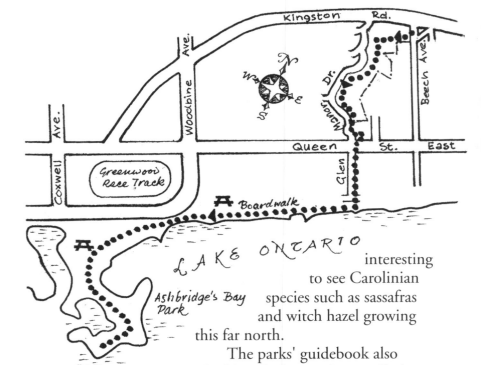

interesting to see Carolinian species such as sassafras and witch hazel growing this far north.

The parks' guidebook also suggests looking for interesting small plants along the banks of the stream, such as coltsfoot and Virginia waterleaf, particularly in spring. (And while the guidebook notes that there used to be a belief that the stream's spring-fed waters had special curative powers, it would probably not be wise to drink the water today.)

At the southerly end of the ravine, the stream disappears underground and the forest gives way to a grassy open area that is being allowed to regenerate naturally. Walkers can continue south along Glen Manor Drive East until reaching a small park just north of Queen on the left-hand side. There are some pretty rockeries in this steep-sided little park. Following the path through it will bring you out to Queen Street.

Cross Queen and continue south on Glen Manor until you come to the Beaches boardwalk. With the destruction of the Sunnyside boardwalk in Toronto's west end in the 1950s, the East Beaches boardwalk has become the stroll of choice for hundreds of Torontonians on Sunday outings and is also used for an annual Easter parade.

Follow the boardwalk west and, when it ends, the paved bicycle path through Beaches Park to Ashbridge's Bay Park. This park has been built on the same kind of construction rubble used to create the nearby Leslie Street Spit, but in contrast to the spit, it has been highly developed and is dominated by a large yacht club. However, if the wind direction is right (away from the nearby sewage treatment plant) and it's a sunny day, it's worth walking out and around the park's headlands for a view of the lake and the city, particularly the leafy Beaches neighbourhood to the east. From Ashbridge's Bay Park, you will have to walk north on Coxwell Avenue to Queen Street to reach a transit stop.

High Park

Everett Hilkers

Colborne Lodge

LENGTH: 5 kilometres
TIME: 1–1 ¹/₂ hours
TERRAIN: Generally flat walking on wide paths with wood-chip or paved surfaces
DIRECTIONS: High Park is located south of Bloor Street, west of Keele Street. From the High Park subway station, walk south 250 metres to the main park entrance. Currently, parking is available in the park, both along park roadways and in a central parking lot at the Grenadier Restaurant. All parking is free. The park is closed to motor vehicle traffic on Sundays and holidays from May to September. As well, car access to the park is currently being reevaluated. While parking is unlikely to be eliminated entirely, it may be greatly reduced in future.

For many Torontonians, High Park is a pleasant green space with big trees, lots of activity and lots of room to wander. What most don't realize is that the park also contains some prime examples of provincially significant ecosystems that are battling both neglect and previously misguided human intervention.

High Park, as anyone who has climbed up to the centre of the park from the south entrance knows, sits generally on high ground—to be exact, on the old Lake Iroquois sand plain. The high, dry ground combined with sandy soils led to the natural development of a savannah treed with black oak, and about a quarter of the park still fits this description. This savannah-type forest, characterized by widely spaced trees and an understorey of mostly prairie plants, is considered rare in Ontario. There are few, if any, places in the greater Toronto area where you will see such a community outside of the park.

Our walk starts at the park's main entrance, off Bloor Street. As you enter the park, turn east (left) and pick up the informal dirt path running from the roadway past the High Park Forest School and toward the eastern slope of the park. This path cuts right through what should be a prime example of oak savannah. The oaks are still here, but due to years of mowing and seeding, the drought-resistant prairie plants that should be growing in their shadows have been replaced with non-native turf. As part of a new ecological approach to the management of the park, however, mowing in much of this area has now stopped. The park staff is hoping that this, combined possibly with the reseeding of prairie species once common to dry areas of Ontario, will help bring this section closer to its natural state.

As you head down the slope, make a quick left and then a right to link up with the wood-chip path that runs north-south, generally following the line of Spring Creek. Looking up, you'll see that you are still surrounded by oaks, but red oaks, which appreciate the greater moisture of the lower slope. Also look for black cherry and red maple, which have similar preferences.

Keep following the wood-chip path south and bear left at each of the two forks you come to. You will pass through a couple of mixed stands of red oak and hemlock. It's also not hard to find Norway maples, one of the scourge species of

High Park and the Toronto ravines. Introduced as a hardy landscaping and street tree, the Norway maple has proved in many places to be too hardy, turning entire areas into Norway maple monocultures that, because little can grow in the deep shade of their dense canopy, often cause severe erosion problems. Part of High Park's proposed management plan is the selective removal and control of species such as Norway maple and Siberian elm.

As you pass another open, oak-and-prairie section along this path you might want to think about another management tool the park staff is proposing to use—fire. Prairie plants, such as little bluestem, wild lupine, pasture rose and sassafras, require periodic fire, both to put nutrients back into the soil and to cut down woody competitors. Without fire (or, less effectively, mowing), prairie becomes forest and, as the prairie disappears, the birds and butterflies that were drawn to the prairie plants disappear, too.

When you reach the bottom of Deer Pen Road, cross over and take the wooden footbridge on your right. Climb up the hill and walk around the washrooms to Colborne Lodge Drive, the park's main road. On the west side of the road and a little to the south, you will see a memorial to John Howard and his wife, Joanna Frances. (Horse chestnuts line the lawn on either side.) A little further south along the east side of the road is Colborne Lodge, the residence the city surveyor built in 1837 (and one of the first homes in the city to have indoor plumbing). Howard, a devout temperancer, deeded 66 hectares of his land to the city in 1873 for use as a public park. The city subsequently acquired land to the east in 1876 from the Rideout family and then the area surrounding and including Grenadier Pond in 1930 from the Chapman Estate.

You can stop for a tour of Colborne Lodge or continue the walk by picking up the wood-chip path running back down the eastern slope from the east side of the utility building next to the lodge. When you reach the paved path at the bottom of the slope, turn right toward the lake and follow it around to Grenadier Pond.

If you had followed this route to the pond in 1837, you would have found yourself virtually standing on the shore of Lake Ontario; only a sandbar separated the pond from the lake then. Gradually the lake was filled, however, first to make way for the Grand Trunk Railroad, then for Lake Shore Boulevard, followed eventually, of course, by the Gardiner Expressway and the Queensway. The water from Grenadier Pond now flows through a storm sewer to reach the lake.

Following the pond's east shore to the north, you'll probably pass a number of people fishing. Amazingly, the pond supports seventeen species of fish, including crappies, carp and largemouth bass. There's no doubt, however, that while progress has been made in restoring the pond's water quality in recent years, more needs to be done. The pond is highly eutrophic, meaning the presence of too many nutrients is sapping the pond's oxygen supply, which in turn leads to algae blooms, discolouration and odours. Park management suggests that lowering the pond's water level and expanding the marshes at its north end would help the

43

water quality. In the longer term, cleaning up the water coming into the pond through storm sewer outfalls is the real answer.

After you've passed the tall marshes at the pond's north end, now frequented by many water birds, the path will veer away from the pond and up into the woods. Follow the lower path along the slope through a mixed forest dominated by oak, and you'll come out on Bloor Street. Take the stairs that lead back into the park from the starting point of the nature trail. Cut across the open area past the playground in a southeasterly direction, cross the road and follow the path past the swimming pool. Cross the next roadway and you'll see a paved path heading east. The area to the south of the path is in the process of being restored to create High Park's "Great Meadow." Head generally south through the meadow, past the step-training fitness station and you'll eventually end up at the allotment gardens. Have a look at some of the gardening techniques (including compost piles and companion plantings to discourage pests) and then head back the way you came on the trail running along the west edge of the gardens. After passing a Y junction on the wood-chip path you're following, you'll come to an intersection with a paved path. Take this path up the hill (past a stand of white spruce) and, when you see the tennis courts, leave the path and walk back through the oak savannah to the park entrance.

Highland Creek

Event hikers.

LENGTH: 12 kilometres
TIME: 4 hours
TERRAIN: Flat
DIRECTIONS: Take the Scarborough RT line to the Midland station. Walk south on Midland to Ellesmere and east 2 1/2 blocks on Ellesmere to the entrance to Birkdale Ravine. If you come by car, you may be able to find parking along Ellesmere. From the end point of the walk at Kingston Road (not Old Kingston Road), take the Scarboro 86 bus west to Warden station. Most walkers will probably prefer to take the bus for the stretch between Markham Road and Morningside Park, during which the walking route follows Lawrence Avenue.

This route takes walkers through both formal parkland and areas that are "wild in the city." Those looking for a shorter trek could start the walk halfway, at the entrance to Morningside Park where Lawrence Avenue East crosses Highland Creek. But if the weather is good and you have your walking shoes on, it's worth taking it from the top, if only to see the contrasts between the manicured parks at the start and the naturalized parks that the route's second half passes through.

Birkdale Ravine is what most of us grew up thinking of as a proper park—green lawns, paved paths and trees scattered here and there, well apart from each other. While sections of the bank have been allowed to sprout some wilder growth, for the most part the park staff keeps the grass mown right to the edge of the creek. Walking through this pleasant if a bit sterile park you'll also work your way around a number of storm sewer outfalls which feed unfiltered water directly—and in high volumes during and after storms—into the creek. The only real inkling you have that you are walking on bottom land here is the occasional bit of squishy turf underfoot.

Just before Brimley Road, however, there is a nice stand of cottonwoods and silver maples tucked into a big bend on the creek, and on the opposite side of the creek, a more natural order often prevails also, which is all the more reason to walk along the grass at the creek edge rather than along the paved path.

Crossing directly over Brimley Road into Thomson Memorial Park, walkers enter a profusion of growth. (This section may be quite wet in the spring, in which case you can walk south on Brimley and enter the park on the opposite side of the creek, on higher ground.) This low-lying wedge of land is bristling with shrub thickets, a dense stand of poplars and even a small marsh, complete with cattails. Follow the grass path through the centre and up the stairs. At the top of the stairs, pause to look at the planting sites on your left and straight ahead. Rather than your usual park garden of petunias and daffodils, these plots have been planted with a mixed community of woody species, including red oak, white pine, dogwood, sumac and speckled alder. It could be worth doing this walk each year just to see how these plots and the area at the bottom of the stairs develop.

Cross over the paved path at the top of the stairs and continue down along the creek. A little further on, there are a couple of picnic shelters and scattered tables. Also along this stretch is a healthy stand of eastern white cedar mixed with white elm. Just before the next footbridge, take the informal path that branches to the left and continue on the east side of the creek. This path will lead you through a pleasant stand of maples and then a lower, shrubbier forest, where you should continue to bear generally right, following the direction of the creek. This soft path will bring you back out to the groomed parkland just before another footbridge. Join up with the paved path and continue under the road bridge. Just a short way after the underpass, look for a small area of cattails and silver maple seedlings on your left. Notice how drainage for this wet depression has been created by using gravel surface channels instead of underground pipes. This way, the water has a chance to filter through the ground and feed gradually into the creek, instead of gushing out after every rainstorm.

Continue to follow the paved path across the first footbridge and under the next overpass. When you reach a path junction, turn left and cross the footbridge. At the next junction, turn right and cross the next footbridge. On the other side, angle across the open area toward an opening in the cedar woods directly in front of you. Follow the soft path through the woods as it bends first right and then left. The path will lead you out to Markham Road. Here, access to the valley is blocked by the Scarborough Golf and Country Club. You will have to walk north to Lawrence (two long blocks), where you can hop a Lawrence East 54E or 54D bus for a five-minute ride east to Morningside Park. Get off at the far end of the long bridge east of Orton Park Road. Cross Lawrence to the north side and descend into the valley on the paved path.

From here on, your surroundings are significantly different. Mown grass has been replaced by meadows, and lollipop trees by mixed stands of maple, birch, oak, cedar and elm. Soon the only sound is rushing water. Just after a life-ring station along the paved path, a dirt path leads off to the left through the woods and along the river. Near the confluence of the Highland and a tributary creek, the dirt path rejoins the paved path, which continues over a concrete bridge. As you enter Colonel Danforth Park, the area's "wildness" is limited to the creek's edge, which you can follow on a dirt path. You will have to abandon the dirt path, however, before it leads you to a low swampy area bisected by a small stream.

From the end of the formal park area, the paved path continues onto the grounds of the University of Toronto's Scarborough Campus. Just inside the boundary is a large meadow bordered by a cedar and hemlock woods. Keep walking straight ahead on the paved path and along the creek and through the campus grounds until you leave the campus and come to Old Kingston Road. Follow the path under the bridge and then around to the right. Cross the creek on the Old Kingston Road

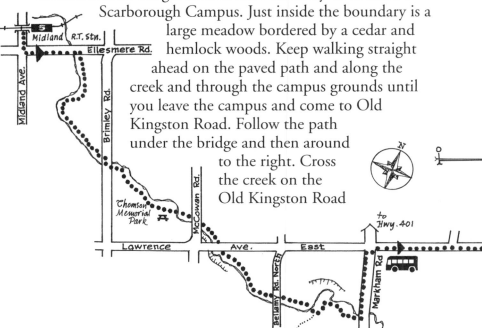

48

bridge and then continue southeast on the path that now runs along the east bank. The path crests a pretty knoll covered with maple and oak trees and then runs under Kingston Road into a small manicured park, where there are washrooms and a pay phone. This is the easiest point from which to leave the valley. Simply walk up the roadway that leads into the park from Kingston Road.

From the parking lot at the south end of the park, however, there is an informal path that continues south to Lawrence Avenue. Exiting the valley at Lawrence means a steep climb up an ungroomed embankment, so if you choose to explore the interesting bottomland forests through here, your best bet is to backtrack to Kingston Road. In this area, Highland Creek is quite wide and fast flowing, and the silty ground underfoot attests to its regular flooding of this dense and damp willow, silver maple and aspen forest. Just south of Lawrence, the path runs into the wall of a steep ridge, which should not be climbed. There's no exit from the top or from further south in the valley in any case, so backtrack to Lawrence or Kingston Road.

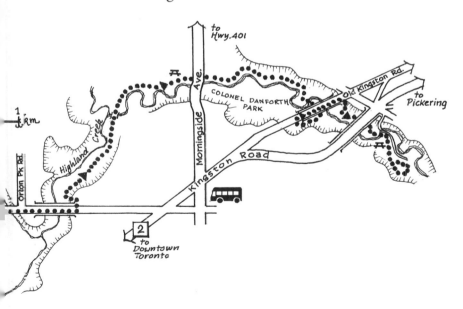

49

Humber Arboretum

Entrance to wild flower garden Arboretum

LENGTH: Approximately 2 kilometres

TIME: 1 ¹/₂–2 hours

TERRAIN: Flat. There are trail signs, but no blazes. Trail surfaces include asphalt, gravel, grass and dirt. Wear boots in the spring and after heavy rains to take full advantage of the trail system. There are lots of benches, picnic tables and a couple of gazebos.

DIRECTIONS: From Highway 27, turn west onto Humber College Boulevard and then south on Arboretum Drive (first left). Drive past college parking to free car park at the Arboretum itself.

Caution: In the past five years, there have been a handful of attacks on women in the vicinity of Humber College. The arboretum staff strongly suggest that women do not walk alone on the grounds.

At 120 hectares, the Humber Arboretum dwarfs your average city park. The space has been used in a variety of ways, from ponds and meadows to lawns and landscaping demonstration gardens. The arboretum's trail system consists of a series of interconnected loops, so walkers can wander as much or as little as they want. By 1992, work had started on extending the Lower Riverside Trail under Highway 427 to the Claireville Conservation Area, which will add another leg-stretching option for visitors. Birders looking for a city outing should in particular consider the Humber Arboretum. Its staff have compiled a list of one hundred species spotted on the grounds since 1981, including a good variety of meadow birds, more than a dozen different warblers and a good selection of raptors, including red-shouldered hawks and great horned owls.

Starting from the nature centre, walk west on the mown grass trail behind the centre; there will be woods on your left and a meadow on your right. Enter the woods and, at the first trail junction, go right to the viewing platform on Oxbow Pond. Water birds, such as herons, mallards and green-winged teal, can often be seen enjoying the arboretum's ponds. Leaving the platform, turn south toward the Humber River. This is the west branch of the river, which, along with the Don, was one of the two main travel arteries for natives and trappers in the Toronto area in earlier times. The Humber is also one of the few rivers in the Toronto area that doesn't draw its waters from the Oak Ridges Moraine. Rather, the river starts as feeder streams on the Niagara Escarpment, an equally delicate—and pressured—ecosystem.

From the riverside gazebo, turn left on Beech Vista Trail to return to the nature centre or continue on Lower

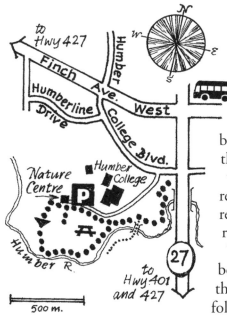

Riverside Trail. A ways further along, you'll come to a footbridge over the Humber River. Cross over and follow the trail in the direction you've come along the opposite bank into a large meadow that offers good bird-watching. When you're ready to leave the meadow, return over the bridge and rejoin the Riverside Trail. The next junction, just before the highway, is with the paved bicycle path that follows the the river east to Islington Avenue. Stay in the arboretum, however, by turning left and walking up a hill past a large pond to the landscaping demonstration gardens. These gardens offer some secluded nooks for picnicking.

Once you've had your fill of the demonstration gardens, return down the hill to the Lower Riverside Trail and turn right. Turn right again at the bridge and climb the stairs to the upper trail. Follow it behind the student residences to the three ponds in front of the nature centre. Before you return to your car, take the time to explore the Toronto Garden Club's wildflower garden. Take the Trillium Trail south to the boardwalk, cross the boardwalk and then return to the nature centre via the Meadow Garden Trail or loop back around the ponds in a counterclockwise direction. The wildflower gardens will be at their best in the spring, but at any time of year they are a great place to get ideas for your own humble yard.

Humber Valley

H umber

Stone bridge at The Old Mill
Étienne Brulé Park.

LENGTH: 9 kilometres
TIME: 2 ½ hours
TERRAIN: Flat. The route follows a paved path or roadway from end to end.
DIRECTIONS: You may have difficulty finding parking near Eglinton and Scarlett Road and, as this is a one-way walk, you might wish to take the TTC in any case. There is parking off Lake Shore Boulevard along Sunnyside Beach near where the Humber trail links into the Martin Goodman Trail. By transit, take the Scarlett 79 bus from Runnymede station to the corner of Scarlett and Eglinton. From the end point of the walk, you can take the 501 streetcar east on the Queensway all the way downtown or transfer onto the 504 streetcar at Roncesvalles Avenue and ride it north to the Dundas West station.

Before the 1800s, travellers or traders arriving at Toronto and intent on heading further north were not greeted by a thriving metropolis complete with coach and rail lines offering their services; rather they faced the daunting prospect of a 30-kilometre portage up the Humber River. From the top of the Humber, it was down the Holland River to Lake Simcoe and then from Simcoe to Georgian Bay and northwest from there.

The route had been established, of course, by the First Nations, who also gave the flat clay plain extending from the Humber to the Don its name—Toronto—which has been interpreted both as carrying place and meeting place. Elizabeth Simcoe, wife of the first lieutenant governor, recorded in her diary a meeting with First Nations representatives who had travelled down the Humber to visit the new settlers and who invited them in turn to visit "our land" to the north.

Provisioning for a trip north certainly shouldn't have been a problem. Before being filled in for various industrial developments over the last hundred years, the Humber Bay marshes on Lake Ontario were renowned for the wildlife, particularly birds, to be found in them. The river itself ran thick with salmon until the mid-1800s.

In historical times, the Humber was a powerful river with many rapids, which necessitated the long portage. The last time the river lashed out, during Hurricane Hazel in 1954, eighty people lost their lives. Since then, the Metropolitan Toronto and Region Conservation Authority has acquired much of the land in the river's flood plain and has installed dams and other waterworks to control its flow.

If this walk suffers from a single problem, it is the manicured park setting that dominates along the Humber. However, both Lambton Woods and what remains of the Humber marshes easily make it a trip worth taking.

Starting at the southeast corner of Eglinton and Scarlett Road, follow the bicycle path south above the river. The bank between the path and the river does have a natural feel to it, and gradually the path pulls away from busy Scarlett Road. The river makes a turn, however, and crosses under Scarlett, as does the bicycle path. Be sure to watch out for speeding cyclists while crossing under the bridge.

On the other side of Scarlett, the path continues through a large open area and then passes a set of tennis courts. Just on the other side of these are a few pockets of wild growth.

Continuing to follow the river closely, the path then leads up a short set of stairs and through a landscaped grove of hemlocks and red pine. After crossing a small brick bridge over a tributary stream, the path leads into Lambton Woods, named for the Lambton Mill which once stood nearby. (By 1860 there were ninety mills operating along the Humber River.) A set of steps on your right leads off the bicycle path to an interesting path that winds through the woods before rejoining the paved path just before the railway trestle.

Take some time to explore this rich woodland. Among the notable tree species to found in it are tamaracks, a more northerly species of conifer and one of the few that loses its needles in winter just as more commonly known broad-leaf deciduous trees lose theirs. As well as other deciduous species such as sugar maple, red oak, blue beech and black cherry, Lambton Woods also contains a small remnant of cedar bog.

And with such a rich overstorey, it's not surprising that the woods have an interesting understorey as well. Among the shrubs, look in particular for witch hazel, a plant with many traditional uses.

From the woods, the bike path continues under the railway trestle and across a large footbridge spanning the Humber. This is a good place to look down the valley and consider what it would be like to portage a canoe up it!

From here south to Bloor Street, the sides of the Humber Valley remain thickly treed and in a mostly natural state, although the flood plain itself is quite open. A short way after you've crossed to the east bank, the bike path makes a turn

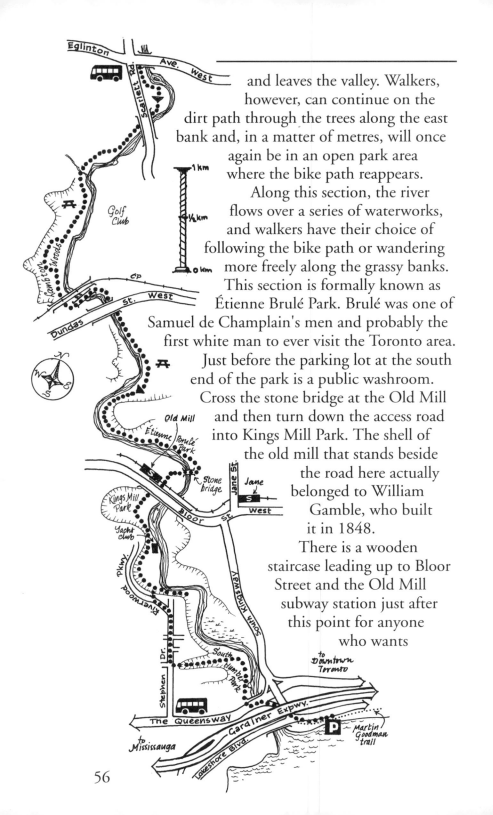

and leaves the valley. Walkers, however, can continue on the dirt path through the trees along the east bank and, in a matter of metres, will once again be in an open park area where the bike path reappears. Along this section, the river flows over a series of waterworks, and walkers have their choice of following the bike path or wandering more freely along the grassy banks. This section is formally known as Étienne Brulé Park. Brulé was one of Samuel de Champlain's men and probably the first white man to ever visit the Toronto area. Just before the parking lot at the south end of the park is a public washroom. Cross the stone bridge at the Old Mill and then turn down the access road into Kings Mill Park. The shell of the old mill that stands beside the road here actually belonged to William Gamble, who built it in 1848.

There is a wooden staircase leading up to Bloor Street and the Old Mill subway station just after this point for anyone who wants to cut the walk short. Otherwise, continue through Kings Mill Park. At the south end, follow the bike path over a small hill and down past the Humber Bay Yacht Club. Because of the way in which the Humber Valley's high sides pinch in here, you'll have to leave the valley for a bit and do some road walking. Follow the roadway that leads from the yacht club south out of the valley to Riverwood Parkway. Turn left and walk to the first intersection. Turn right on Stephen Drive and walk south past a set of traffic lights until, on the east side of the roadway, you see the entrance to South Humber Park.

The path into the South Humber takes you along a tributary stream and then into an open grassy area next to the river. If you walk into the woods behind the restroom/ shelter building located here, you can find a couple of good spots for looking out on the marshes that dot the meandering river through this stretch.

A large concern of naturalists is whether these marshes are collecting contaminants spilled into the river by industry as well as from run-off from roads and through storm sewer outfalls. Nesting and visiting waterfowl, they fear, could be poisoned by eating fish and other aquatic material that has in turn fed on contaminated organisms lower down in the food chain. When this happens, species higher up in the food chain bio-accumulate dangerous levels of toxins in their systems. If we ever want to see rivers like the Humber teeming with salmon and waterfowl again, we are going to have do something about issues such as these.

If you've had your fill of marsh walking, you can continue to follow the path around the Humber Sewage Treatment Plant (don't worry, it's hidden from sight) and out to the Queensway. At this point you have a choice of continuing on the path down to Lake Shore Boulevard, where it joins up with the Martin Goodman Trail, or of walking across the north side of the Queensway Bridge and from there crossing to the streetcar loading platform on the Queensway.

If you want to continue, just follow the signs for the Martin Goodman Trail. Once you've reached Lake Shore, High Park is less than a kilometre to the east. After that, your next transit access point would be the bottom of Roncesvalles Avenue, which you can reach by crossing the pedestrian footbridge located in front of the Palais Royal dance hall.

Jack Darling Memorial Park and Rattray Marsh

Rattray Marsh

LENGTH:
Approximately 2 kilometres
TIME: 1 ¹/₂–2 hours
TERRAIN: Flat
DIRECTIONS: The park is located on the waterfront in Mississauga, on the south side of Highway 2 (Lake Shore Road West) approximately 2.5 kilometres west of Mississauga Road. There's free parking at the park. By transit, take Mississauga Transit's Lake Shore 23 West bus from the Port Credit GO station to the park entrance.

This walk explores just a tiny fragment of the Lake Ontario waterfront that lies within the boundaries of the Greater Toronto Area. However, one of the key recommendations of the Crombie Commission on the Future of Toronto's Waterfront was the development of a waterfront greenway from Burlington in the west to Port Hope in the east. The idea of a greenway is to develop something that is more than a trail; it should be a natural habitat corridor that aids the

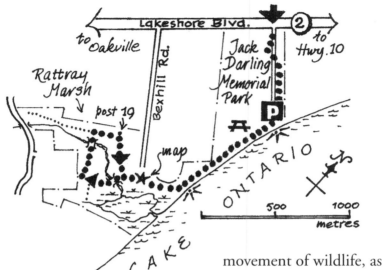

movement of wildlife, as
well as people. Along the way
would be "green nodes," larger
green areas such as High Park or the Rouge Valley Park that
will be easily accessible from the greenway and provide refuge
for wildlife. Granted, there's a long way to go from a small
section of trail such as the one found in Jack Darling to a
watershed-spanning corridor like the one proposed by the
Crombie Commission, but work is already underway on a
Mississauga waterfront trail, the first section of which, from
the Credit River to Marie Curtis Park in Etobicoke, could
open as early as some time in 1993.

For now, however, enter Jack Darling Park at the
signed entrance and walk across the lawn under the willow
trees to the lake. Before continuing west, take a minute to
catch the view of the Toronto cityscape to the east. Then
follow the shoreline away from the city to Rattray Marsh.

Follow the gravel trail into the marsh and turn left for
another good view of the lake or turn right to view a map of
the marsh trails. Be sure to have binoculars handy, because
this is a good spot for bird-watching. After you've toured

the marsh, you might also just want to sit and watch the lake for a while.

A nice loop of the marsh can be done by walking straight ahead at the trail sign, across Sheridan Creek to the far edge of the marsh. Here you'll turn right into a pleasant woodlot of poplar and black cherry trees. At the next trail junction, turn right again and follow the trail behind some large homes. At a brown post with a 19 clearly marked on the top, turn right again to return to the gravel trail that brought you into the marsh. Turn left and return to Jack Darling Park.

Kortright Centre for Conservation

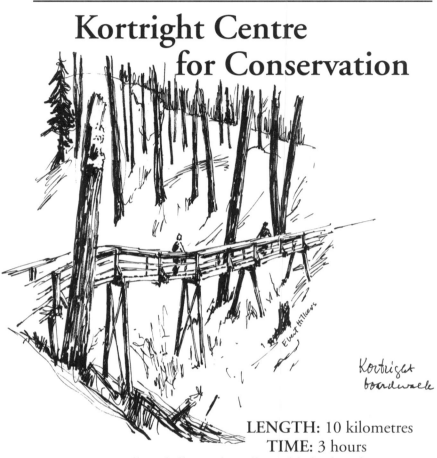

Kortright boardwalk

LENGTH: 10 kilometres
TIME: 3 hours
TERRAIN: Rolling hills, with well-established paths
DIRECTIONS: Take Highway 400 to Major Mackenzie Drive (the turnoff for Canada's Wonderland). Drive west three kilometres to Pine Valley Drive, then south one kilometre to the centre's entrance.

The Kortright Centre is more than a place to walk; it's a place to learn. With Canada's largest staff of professional naturalists, Kortright is about interpreting—and enjoying—the wonders of nature. The site itself consists of 162 hectares of diverse, undisturbed natural habitat, ranging from forested tablelands to meadows and swamps to river valleys. You can explore it on your own or you can join in on one of the more than five hundred planned activities—from pond studies to bird-feeder building—held at Kortright each year.

The trails within the centre consist of a series of loops, so you can fit your walk to a preferred distance and to your interests. It's possible to walk from Kortright to the McMichael Gallery in Kleinburg, but because the trail crosses land leased out to a farmer by the conservation authority, you'll have to wait until the centre puts on a guided walk to reach the gallery from here. Trails within the centre are not blazed, but have posts with letters that will help you orient yourself on the centre's map.

Start off from the visitor's centre, set on a ravine crest in a beautiful hardwood forest. (Inside the centre are displays and a theatre, as well as information on demonstrations and guided walks.) From the centre, walk west and slightly south on the Forestry Path, which passes through a mature forest with some very healthy sugar maples and white pines. Many other trees are labelled, so this is a good place to practise your tree identification skills. The trail emerges from the woods and skirts the edge of a meadow that holds lots of promise for butterfly watchers before reaching a Y junction. From the junction, continue south along the meadow edge and then east, crossing the main access road before turning north. Bear right as the trail takes you over Marigold Creek and along the western edge of Pine Valley Drive. The path crosses the creek again and then turns east.

At the next trail junction, make a side trip down to Spring Peeper Pond by turning left. After you've had a look around this wetland complex and possibly heard the songs of some peepers, reverse direction at post Q and head back up to the trail junction you came from and turn left. To get away from some of the noise of Major Mackenzie Drive, turn left again at the second trail junction you come to (post N). This trail will take you through an interesting area that has been planted with shrubs to provide shelter and food for birds and other wildlife.

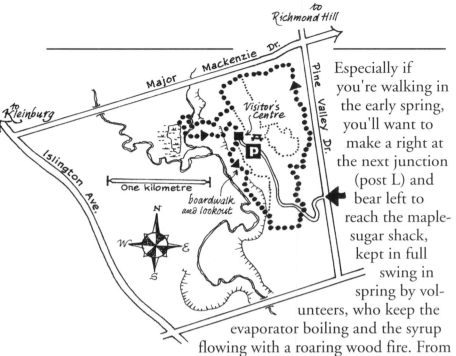

Especially if you're walking in the early spring, you'll want to make a right at the next junction (post L) and bear left to reach the maple-sugar shack, kept in full swing in spring by volunteers, who keep the evaporator boiling and the syrup flowing with a roaring wood fire. From the sugar shack, continue south to post I, where you make a sharp right to take a trail leading you along the edge of, and then through, a wood as you drop down toward Cold Creek.

At the next junction (post H), turn right and cross the creek before reaching another junction. Turn right again and follow the boardwalk through the marsh to the viewing tower. There's usually lots of bird and aquatic life to be seen in the swamp, so take your time and watch closely. From the viewing tower, continue south, keeping right at the various intersections. The trail now takes you down along the edge of the East Humber River, and various aspects of river life are explained by displays along the way. Keep right as you follow the trail west and it leaves the river, once again coming up to the sugar bush before passing through to post E. From here, turn right and head back to the visitors centre.

If you still have some energy, finish your day with a loop around the Power Trip Trail. This path runs past a number of alternative energy displays, ranging from home conservation techniques to solar and wind-power generators. These recently rebuilt displays are well worth a look.

Leslie Street Spit
(Tommy Thomson Park)

LENGTH: 10–15 kilometres
TIME: 3–4 hours
TERRAIN: There is only one steep grade on the spit, approximately at its midpoint. Otherwise, it is flat. A paved road runs the length of the spit, making it fully wheelchair accessible. Public access to the park is limited to weekends and holidays (except Christmas and New Year's), nine a.m to six p.m. Dogs are not allowed.
DIRECTIONS: During June, July and August, there is TTC service to the spit from the corner of Berkshire and Queen streets every hour, starting at 8:45 a.m. In other months, take

the Jones 83 bus south from Donlands station to Commissioners Street and then follow the Martin Goodman Trail south along the east side of Leslie Street to the spit. The Metropolitan Toronto and Region Conservation Authority runs a minibus service up and down the spit itself from late spring to roughly Thanksgiving. Call (416) 661-6000 for schedule. There is space for a few cars to park at the base of the spit.

The Leslie Street Spit has become renowned as one of the prime wildlife viewing areas in Toronto, which, considering its industrial beginnings, may at first seem somewhat surprising. The spit began as a project of the Toronto Harbour Commission in the 1950s. The plan was to create a new outer harbour to accommodate the increased ship traffic expected to result from the construction of the St. Lawrence Seaway. Of course, ship traffic declined rather than increased, and the harbour commission, recognizing it had no real use for the 5-kilometre-long rubble pile it had created, turned the spit over to the Metropolitan Toronto and Region Conservation Authority (MTRCA).

Since then, as trucks continue to rumble down Leslie Street to dump loads of construction waste on the spit, a natural evolution has occurred on those parts that are no longer in active use. But while pioneer plant species have quietly gone about establishing themselves, a noisy battle has raged between those who favour building large marinas and other facilities on the spit and those who favour leaving it virtually undeveloped. MTRCA's current master plan for the spit leans toward making it an undeveloped nature reserve.

As a nature reserve, the spit has a lot to offer. Close to four hundred species of plants, some of them rare in Ontario, have been identified. The spit is widely acknowledged to be a birder's paradise, as well, with 285 bird species having been identified there.

In constructing the spit, the engineers created an outer rim of large rubble and rock, which in turn is filled with finer sand and gravel. This has resulted in soil conditions that are very similar to those of the nearby Toronto Islands, and wind-blown seed from the Islands (particularly cottonwood seeds) are probably a significant source for the plant life that has developed on the spit. Currently, construction work continues on the east side of the spit, and this area is officially out of bounds, even on weekends. Three "cells" have been created along the east side of the spit to hold silt dredged from the Keating Channel and other areas of the harbour. As this silt contains varying levels of heavy metals, the cells are not open to the lake and will eventually be capped with clay, after which the plan is to try to develop wetland communities on each of them. The creation of a marsh in cell one may begin in 1993.

A paved road runs from the base of the spit right to the lighthouse at its southern tip. Walking on the spit is a matter of heading as far down the road as you like and detouring onto each or any of the four peninsulas that extend west from it. Your decision on what peninsulas to visit may in part be dictated by the season and by what you're interested in seeing.

It's important to remember that there has been no human intervention in establishing habitat on the spit. Rather, this is a true successional community, with tough weedy species such as silverweed, clover, wild carrot, fleabane and ragweed creating conditions that other species can exploit. The clovers (yellow flowering in late spring and the more common white flowering in early summer) are particularly important, as they have the ability to fix nitrogen in the spit's poor soil.

The successional process is furthest along on peninsulas D and C, toward the base of the spit. These areas are covered in a mixture of scrub and immature woodland. The scrub is mostly sandbar willows, while in the woodlands, the dominant tree is eastern cottonwood, interspersed with other poplars and aspens. For the most part, the understorey for these woodlands consists of sandbar willow and red-osier dogwood. However, keep an eye out for showy lady's-slipper growing under the cottonwoods that line the main roadway.

One of the more unusual plants to be found on the spit is the prickly pear cactus, found on peninsula C. It's unclear how this particular plant came to be established on the spit, but the sheltered spot it has chosen is probably critical to the survival of this nationally endangered species.

On peninsulas A and B, large colonies of gulls are at least partly responsible for holding back natural plant succession. As many as fifty thousand ringbill gull nests can be found on the spit in any given year. The gulls find the spit's open rocky shoreline exactly to their liking, and their sheer numbers suffocate much plant life. Terns, in contrast, have been virtually pushed off the spit by the gulls. The Canadian Wildlife Service has stepped in on their behalf and built nesting rafts for the terns to use just offshore of the spit. The rafts are so popular that the terns now wheel overhead as the rafts are being towed into position each spring.

The spit is also a nesting spot for about two thousand black-crowned night herons. These birds can be a good deal harder to find than the gulls, but try looking for their stick nests in trees on peninsula C in May before the trees are in leaf.

The best time to see non-nesting birds on the spit is probably the fall, when many species will stop for a few days or more to rest and feed before continuing their southward migration. Meanwhile, late August to early September is the time to see migrating monarch butterflies, which stop on the spit to gather nectar from goldenrod and asters. The best areas for monarch watching are south of the swing bridge.

And don't forget about the spit in winter (but dress warmly). Due to the moderating influence of the lake, plants are often still green and growing on the spit long after the rest of the Toronto landscape has become brown and dormant. In particular, low-lying areas on peninsula B create a warm microclimate that allows some plants to flower right into the early winter. As well, keep an eye out for snowy owls, which in turn, will be keeping an eye out for mice and voles.

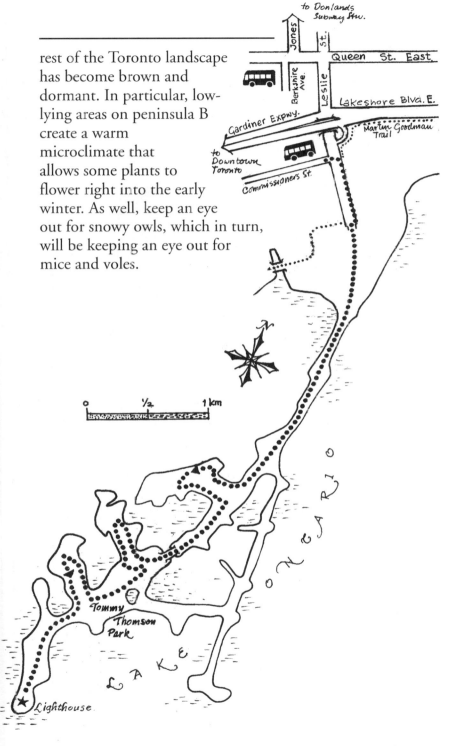

Rosedale Ravine

Rosedale Ravine — Balfour Park.

LENGTH: 8 kilometres
TIME: 2 hours
TERRAIN: Mostly flat walking, with a couple of steep grades and steep staircases to climb
DIRECTIONS: By TTC, the walk begins and ends at Summerhill subway station. By car, park toward the end of Shaftesbury Avenue or park in a public lot at Yonge and Summerhill or Yonge and St. Clair and start the walk either from the end of Shaftesbury Avenue or from the Mount Pleasant Cemetery gates.

Montreal may have Mount Royal, and Vancouver may have Stanley Park, but Toronto has its system of ravines and river valleys. This system of green corridors, which penetrates right to the core of the city, contributes much to Toronto's reputation as a green and treed city. One of the most "downtown" ravine addresses is the Rosedale Ravine system, and using it in combination with the Mount Pleasant Cemetery and the Don Valley to create a loop in the north-central part of the city, we get a walk that puts us in touch with the natural and human history of Toronto.

From the Summerhill subway station follow Shaftesbury Avenue east. At the end of the street is a gravel path with a sign directing walkers to a nature trail. The trail leads down into the ravine through stands of mature maple, oak and black cherry trees. When the trail reaches the path running alongside the creek, turn north and continue on the west side of the creek past the green wooden footbridge. The creek running through this ravine is deeply shaded by natural growth, but for the most part, it's also channelized with large stone blocks—the result of sewer work done in the 1960s.

Continue on the path as it begins to climb higher up the west side of the ravine. On the slope beneath the path, you will pass a number of standing dead trees—known by foresters as snags—more than one of which has had holes and cavities opened up in it by woodpeckers. Snags are an important element in a mature forest because of the shelter they provide for cavity nesters, such as the seldom-seen eastern bluebird and small mammals such as squirrels. Because old, decaying trees are quickly removed in the city, species such as bluebirds have become rare in our parks and ravines.

After you've limbered up your legs climbing almost to the top of the western edge of the ravine, you will see a staircase leading back down to your right. Take the staircase and follow the path as it leads under the St. Clair Avenue bridge. Be careful walking under the bridge and on the far side; there is loose stone here.

The path continues along the west bank of the creek until you reach the southern boundary of Mount Pleasant Cemetery. There are gates into the cemetery and, if they're open, take this route in. If the gates are locked, take the staircase leading out of the ravine on your left, in the direction of Yonge Street. At the top of the stairs, continue west on Heath Street to the first cross street, Alvin Avenue. Turn right and follow the avenue to Glen Elm Avenue. Turn left and walk out to Yonge. Turn north (right) on Yonge and you will quickly come to a set of brick gates leading into the cemetery.

The history of Toronto can be read in the headstones of this 500-hectare cemetery opened in 1876. Upper Canada's elite are buried here; names such as Moore, Strachan and Dundas are part of the fabric of Toronto to this day, while Eaton and Mackenzie King are known throughout Canada. But just as Mount Pleasant is known for the many famous and important figures buried in its lawns, the cemetery is also renowned for its collection of trees and shrubs; many of the oaks and maples are as stately as any that can be seen anywhere in Toronto. Guides to both who is buried where and to the cemetery plants can be obtained from the cemetery office, located inside the eastern half of the grounds, just off Mount Pleasant Road.

From the gates on Yonge Street, plot your wanderings in a generally northeasterly direction to reach the underpass that runs under Mount Pleasant at the northern edge of the cemetery. Once you've emerged on the eastern side of Mount Pleasant, follow the road around until you reach a landscaped rock-slab pool. Head directly south at this point, crossing the cemetery until you reach a wood-chip path leading in the direction of a gazebo. Follow the path to the gazebo, where you will exit the cemetery.

Directly across Moore Avenue is the entrance to the Moore Park Ravine. This is a narrow ravine with dense growth of young maple and oak trees and lots of shrubs. The appeal of this setting to birds should make this a good spot for bird-watching, especially if you can identify birds by call.

Keep following the rock-chip path as the ravine widens out before it hooks in with the main trunk of the Don Valley. Just as you enter the valley, you will pass the old site of the Don Valley brickworks and the pit from which clay was dug for brick making. After early plans to build luxury housing on the site were scrapped, the brickworks were purchased by the Metro Toronto government in the late 1980s. Part of the argument for public ownership was based on the unique opportunity to study the geological history of Toronto by studying the layers of sedimentation and fossils in the old pit face. Currently, however, there is no public access to the site, and as well as being potential parkland, the site is being considered for a police-dog training centre and a works yard.

Just beyond the brickworks as you continue south into the Don Valley, you will pass a steep slope and a dirt path leading up into Chorley Park. Continue straight ahead, though, and follow the main path as it curves to the west along the edge of a highway ramp. Signs at a trail junction will point you toward Balfour Park along a gravel path lined with lampposts. At the foot of the path is a small marshy area that might hold possibilities for amphibian lovers.

Growth through this section is more mature than in the Moore Park Ravine, with healthy stands of shade-loving beech trees standing out on the slopes. A little further along, the path leads gently uphill through an open meadow area, punctuated by a solitary cherry tree. At the top of the hill is a formal parkette with benches to take a rest on.

From the parkette, carefully cross busy Mount Pleasant Road and continue along the path in Balfour Park until the paved path ends at a drinking fountain. Cross the footbridge near the fountain and then turn left and follow the dirt path back in the direction you came along the opposite bank of the creek. When you come to a split in the path near the remains of an old bridge, you've once again reached the base of the trail that led you into the ravine from Shaftesbury Avenue. Follow the path with the handrail back up to Shaftesbury, and Shaftesbury back to the subway station.

Scarborough Bluffs

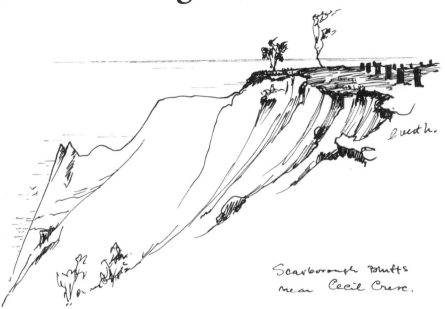

Scarborough Bluffs near Cecil Cresc.

LENGTH: 5 kilometres
TIME: 2 hours
TERRAIN: Mostly flat walking, with a steep descent down to, and a steep climb up from, Bluffer's Park
DIRECTIONS: Take the Kingston Road 12 bus to Birchmount Road. Walk south to Springbank Avenue and then east to the end of Springbank. There is limited curb parking on Springbank.

The Scarborough Bluffs reminded Lady Simcoe, wife of the first lieutenant governor of Upper Canada, of the white cliffs of England. Rising 110 metres (350 feet) from the lake, there is no doubt that the bluffs are one of Toronto's most spectacular geological features—even if, to a less homesick eye, they may appear more grey than white.

The bluffs were actually formed in two stages. The bottom 50 metres, known to geologists as the Scarborough

75

Beds, are what remains of a giant river delta, formed when the lake was 50 metres higher than today. The rest of the work on the bluffs was done by the Wisconsin glacier during the last ice age, some twelve thousand years ago. Four advances and retreats by this sheet of ice left another 60 metres of boulder clay and sand piled on top of the underlying beds. As the lake level dropped, the bluffs were exposed and have been shaped by wind, rain and waves ever since.

The bluffs mark the eastern edge of the flat clay plain that, while somewhat marshy in spots, made Toronto an attractive spot to build a settlement. The city, of course, has long since sprawled past the bluffs and, unfortunately, public access to them is intermittent, thanks to residential development, which in many places has pushed right up to the bluff edge.

Starting from the end of Springbank Avenue, walk into the small pocket park that connects it to Lakehurst Crescent. Here there is a good view of the lake from the bluff edge, especially from the small point that extends out at about the middle of the park. The park itself is notable mostly for a number of large Norway spruce trees, a European species widely planted as an ornamental in Ontario.

From the east edge of the park, follow Lakehurst Crescent to the entrance to Rosetta McClain Gardens. In the gardens, walkers are kept back from the bluff edge by a chain-link fence. The gardens themselves contain a mixture of formal and naturalized gardens, and it's worth taking a spin around the various beds before continuing on. Leave the gardens from the northeast corner by the rose beds and follow Fishleigh Drive east for a short distance. Just before you reach the filtration plant on Fishleigh, follow the edge of a side ravine back to the top edge of the bluffs. (Don't follow the road to the base of the bluffs.)

76

The area around the filtration plant is mostly mown grass, but the bluff edge itself has a thick growth of shrubs, and there are many good viewpoints. Reaching a fence at the eastern edge of the grounds, follow it back to Fishleigh Drive. Because housing has been built to the bluff edge east of here, the next stretch is all road walking.

Follow Fishleigh Drive to Midland Avenue, Midland north to Romana, and Romana east to Scarboro Crescent. At the base of Scarboro Crescent, parkland along the bluffs begins again. There are some good views along here, including overlooks of the man-made Bluffer's Park below and of interesting formations left by the uneven erosion of the bluffs themselves.

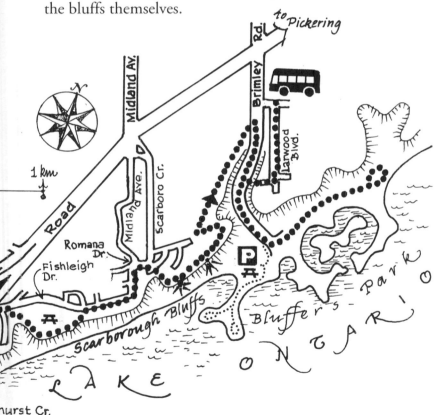

Continue to follow the bluff edge until you come to a small copse of trees that has been heavily eroded by bike riders. Follow the path through the trees and out into an old field area, with a wide, well-defined path running through it. This area is particularly pretty in fall when goldenrod and purple and white asters are blooming in the fields. Follow the path as it makes a large loop through the field and brings you back to a point where a road dead-ends.

From the north side of the roadway, follow the gravel path that leads up through a gully treed with Manitoba maples and then a more mature forest of beech, hemlock and maple. Just before the path ends, turn right and follow the dirt path through the trees and out into another field. Follow the informal paths through this field over to the slope edge above Brimley Road. Turn left and follow the path along the slope edge until you come to a point where the open grassy slope ends and a section of scrubbier slope begins.

At this point, you can follow an old tractor track down the slope to Brimley Road. However, if this looks too slippery or steep for your taste, continue to follow the slope north until you reach a gravel driveway. You will now be separated from Brimley Road by a fence, but there is a pedestrian gate at the north end of the drive.

From whichever point you link up with Brimley Road, follow it down to the lake. It's best to walk on the east shoulder, as cars climbing the hill move a lot slower than some of those descending. This is not the most pedestrian-friendly stretch of road—it has a number of blind spots—so use caution!

When you reach Bluffer's Park at the base of the road, follow the gravel footpath running east behind the boat storage and docking areas. (There are washrooms, pay phones, picnic tables and restaurants in the park.) Eventually, this path will bring you to the beach at the far end of the landfill park. From here, you can follow the beach as far as water levels allow. There are interesting wetland areas behind the beach and, on quiet days, this could be a good place to look for both shorebirds and water birds.

Once you've finished exploring Bluffer's Park, back-track to Brimley and start the long climb back up. About halfway up the hill on your right, you will see an old road allowance (now closed off) running parallel to the slope. Leave Brimley and follow the path along the old roadway and then hook left and climb a short but steep pitch to Redland Crescent.

For one last look at the bluffs, follow the path to the right at the top and circle through the woods on the point. This is a mature pocket of woodland with an interesting mixture of trees, including sugar maple, red oak, birch, white pine, black cherry and bitternut hickory.

Once you've worked your way back to Redland Crescent, walk east to Larwood Boulevard and north on Larwood to Barkdene Hills. From the TTC stop on Barkdene, you can take the Kingston Road 12 bus east to Victoria Park and from there connect to a streetcar to continue east or go north to Victoria Park station.

Seneca College – King Campus

Evert Hillkers

LENGTH: 7 kilometres
TIME: 2 hours
TERRAIN: Rolling hills, with some wet spots
DIRECTIONS: From Highway 400 take King Side
Road east to Dufferin Street. Go north (left) on Dufferin
until you see the signs on your left for Seneca College, King
Campus. Parking is two dollars. Seneca College runs a bus
service from Toronto, but it is only for students.

There is probably no family better known in Canada than
the Eatons of department-store fame. The centrepiece of
Seneca College's King Campus is the one-time home of Flora
Eaton, the daughter-in-law of the department store's
founder, Timothy Eaton. Flora's husband, John "Jack" Craig
Eaton, died of pneumonia in 1922 while the house was still
in the planning stages. The Eatons were apparently con-

vinced to buy the property, which actually consisted of six farms, by their Toronto neighbour Sir Henry Pellatt, the man who constructed Casa Loma.

Prior to the arrival of settlers, the property was apparently crossed by an ancient Indian trail running between Lake Ontario and Lake Simcoe. (Among the evidence for this was the discovery of a dugout canoe by workers restocking the lake for the Eatons.) Construction of the massive stone mansion at the centre of the Seneca property started in 1938 and was finished by 1940, at which point it was turned over to the navy to be used as a convalescent home for injured sailors. Flora Eaton eventually moved into the house in 1949. During her residence, the property continued as a working farm. As well, Lady Eaton saw to the reforestation of a large area of the property to the north and west of Eaton Hall.

The estate was sold to Seneca College in 1961, and Eaton Hall now serves as an executive conference centre and restaurant. The grounds around the home include two small lakes and a variety of natural habitats, from pine plantations to a maple-sugar bush. A full network of cross-country ski trails have been laid out through the woods and fields of the campus, and that means that there are lots of options for walkers in the off-season; this route is just one of them.

Starting off from the parking lot near the gatehouse, follow the road past the log cabin until you reach the intersection of the road and ski trails. Follow the trail to the right past the sugaring-off shack that's the centre of activity in this sugar bush when the sap starts flowing in late February or early March. On leaving the woods, turn right and follow the top edge of the bush and then cut straight across the open field to the tractor path that runs north along an old rail bed. Follow this pine-bordered pathway up the eastern edge of the property all the way to the back fence. This whole corner is rich in conifers, including white pine, red pine and balsam fir, no doubt providing good protection from wind and snow for skiers—and other animals—in winter. Most likely, this area represents old farmland that has been replanted, but for the most part, the look is fairly natural without the regimented rows of some softwood plantations.

When you reach the back fence, turn left and continue straight until you reach the second trail intersection. This stretch includes a large dip that should get your heart pumping on the uphill (and a few skiers' knees knocking on the downhill). At the intersection, turn left and hook back almost in the direction you've come. There's a pleasantly sheltered opening a little ways along here, with some maples, oaks and other deciduous trees providing shade. Follow the trail down and to the right, making a virtual U-turn at the bottom as you come around the curve. When you come to a T intersection, turn left and follow the trail in the direction of the lake. As you emerge

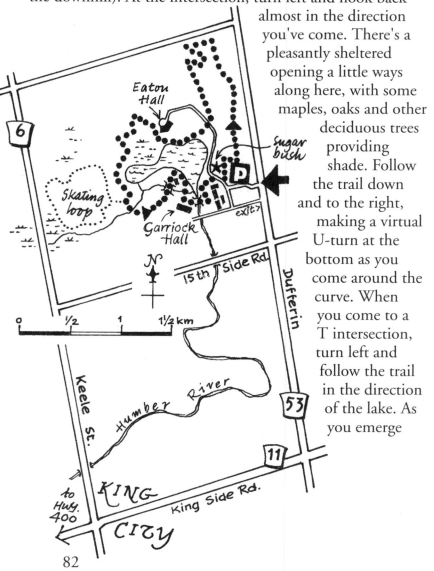

from the trees and get a glimpse of the lake, turn toward it, walking across the road and past the small parking lot. When you reach the lake, turn right and follow the edge. The trail cuts through some small shoreline marshes and the footing can get quite wet, so watch your step. You might want to take advantage of the small gazebo on the lake at the foot of Eaton Hall Hill to take a rest while watching for water birds.

Walk up the hill past the west wing of Eaton Hall and stick with the ski trail as it bends off to the left. A short way from the hall, you'll reach another trail junction marked with a ski trail sign where a narrower path breaks off from the wide path you're following. Turn left and climb up higher into the maple and beech forest that is dominant on this side of the property. This path isn't as wide or flat as the earlier parts, and in low spots, you'll be glad you're wearing boots. As the trail dips up and down, the surrounding vegetation changes with it; from hemlock, cedar and birch in the wetter low-lying areas to sugar maple, beech and oak on the ridges.

Within about a kilometre of entering the deciduous forest, the trail makes a sharp left turn. With Little Lake visible through the dogwood and sumac thickets that line its edge, you'll also notice a number of good-size oaks keeping to the drier, higher ground on the trail's west side. Eventually, the trail leaves the woods and comes out into a section of old field along the lake. The shrub thickets that line the edge of the lake provide good shelter for birds, so bring your binoculars. Your choice now is to continue on the skating loop trail, which circles a tilled field for 2 kilometres, or to start back toward the parking lot.

If you're heading back, from the junction of the skating loop and the main trail, follow the edge of the tall grass in an inverted L until you come to a bridge over a small creek. Cross over and turn left to follow the road leading back toward the walk's starting point. Just before you reach the newly built Garriock Hall, follow the road down toward Little Lake, watching for ducks in the creek. Swing past the maintenance buildings at the bottom of the road and over to the beach and dock on the west shore of Lake Seneca. Behind you is the ski centre, with washrooms and picnic tables. Continue south from the ski centre and over the footbridge in front of Garriock Hall and then turn left and cross the next footbridge before making an immediate left again. Walk up and around the back of the buildings in this area and then past a line of large, mature trees. Notice in particular the black walnut tree, a rare species usually found growing in more southerly areas of the province. In the fall, you'll find the walnuts encased in large green fruit the size of tennis balls. Once past the walnut trees, you're within sight of the parking lot you started off from.

Toronto Islands

Boardwalk to Ward's Island

LENGTH: 9 kilometres
TIME: 3 hours
TERRAIN: Flat
DIRECTIONS: At the Island ferry docks at the foot of Bay Street, board the Hanlan's Point ferry. The Harbourfront LRT extension to the Yonge-University subway will take you almost to the docks (Queen's Quay station). There is ferry service year-round to Hanlan's Point and Ward's Island. Service to Centre Island runs only from late spring to early fall. For schedule and fare information, call (416) 392-8193. During the main season, concessions and washrooms are open in all areas of the Islands. For something other than hotdogs, try the Ward's Island Café, located just south of the ferry docks.

The Islands have been a refuge from the heat and noise of the city since Toronto's earliest days. In fact, Elizabeth Simcoe, wife of the first lieutenant governor of Upper Canada, would probably heartily approve if Torontonians chose to spend their annual August Simcoe Day holiday exploring the Islands; Mrs. Simcoe spent many hours walking on what, in her day, was a sandy peninsula enclosing Toronto's inner harbour.

Of course, a great deal has changed since then. In 1858, a large storm washed away a section of the peninsula to create what is today the eastern gap and, in the process, the Islands. As well, what in the 1800s was an area of meadows, dunes, beaches and cottonwood woodlands has today become almost entirely formal parkland; it is estimated that less than one-eighth of the Islands' total area remains in a natural state.

Various types of development have come and gone on the Islands. Starting in the 1920s, they became a summer retreat and tenting ground for Toronto residents. Gradually, the platforms, sheds and outbuildings built around each tent site evolved into full-scale cottages. Hotels, dance pavilions, amusement parks, and even a full-scale baseball stadium on Hanlan's Point also came and went during the 1900s.

When the island lands were transferred to the newly created Metropolitan Toronto government in the 1950s, a controversial decision was made to remove all residential development on the Islands in favour of open parkland. That decision sparked a twenty-year battle, which eventually ended in the decision to leave what housing remained on Ward's and Algonquin islands untouched.

Geologically, the Islands are a result of sediment eroded from the Scarborough Bluffs being deposited by shore currents in long, thin strands along the outer edge of Toronto's natural harbour.

Vegetation on the Islands (particularly the meadow species) is sensitive to lake levels, notes biologist Steve Varga in *Toronto Islands: Plant Communities and Noteworthy Species* (published by the Toronto Field Naturalists). The remnant natural meadows are usually completely flooded in the spring, he notes, before gradually drying out over the summer months.

86

In drier years when the meadows do not completely flood, the result can be dramatic shifts in their species composition.

This walk stays mostly to the outer edges of the Islands. From the ferry dock at Hanlan's Point, walk south along the path closest to the lagoon edge. After passing the end of the fence enclosing the island airport on your right, start angling west, across the lawn toward the lake and the Islands' western beaches. On warm days, you may prefer to stay back from the beach a bit and walk along the informal paths that crisscross through the grasses and young trees just behind the open sand. Venture out onto the open dune system, however, to take a look at an ecosystem found nowhere else in the Greater Toronto Area. These hot, dry dunes are home to tough pioneer species such as marram grass, Canada wild rye and willow.

The flatter strands of beach in front of the dunes make for equally difficult growing conditions, and most of what grows here are annuals. Which plants will be present in any given year is highly dependent on moisture levels. Varga suggests looking for sedges such as river cyperus, umbrella-sedge and fragrant cyperus in wetter spots and, in drier sections, for bushy cinquefoil, which features five-petalled yellow flowers and is rare elsewhere in the province but grows abundantly here.

Follow the beach around to the east, stopping at Gibraltar Point to explore the large wet meadow just behind the beach. In the meadow, the sedges stick to the shallower edges, while the centre is dominated by spike rush, Baltic rush and Nelson's horsetail. September may be the best time to visit the Gibraltar Point meadow, which should by then be white with nodding ladies' tresses orchids.

From the meadow, continue east, cutting through a dense stand of cottonwood trees before emerging in front of the Island Nature School. Walk on the beach past the school and then past the water filtration plant. Just to the north of the filtration plant is one of the Islands' more extensive natural areas, with a couple of high-quality wet meadows and an extensive eastern cottonwood woodland. Paths through this woodland can require some bushwhacking, as red-osier dogwood and willow shrubs crowd in from all sides.

In the openings made by the wet meadows in these woodlands, you will find small examples of sand prairie ecosystems, featuring prairie grass species such as big bluestem and switch grass. Saw-whet owls are also usually plentiful in these woods during fall migration.

After exploring this area, head back down the path alongside the filtration plant to the lakeshore and continue east along the lakefront path. From the wilds of the Islands' western end, you now enter the heavily built-up Centre Island portion. A series of formal gardens marks the main route that joins Centre Island to a large fishing pier on the lake. Continue east past the Centre Island bathing beaches and then along a concrete sea wall before eventually reaching a boardwalk. Follow the boardwalk past a number of over-

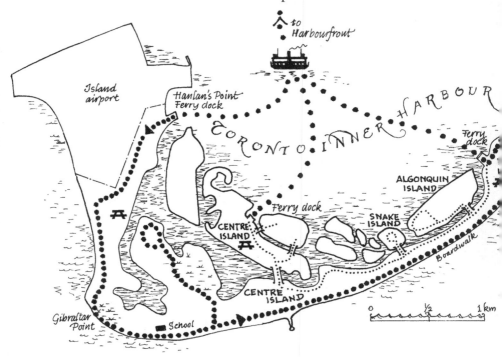

grown foundations (all that's left of the houses removed in the 1950s) all the way to Ward's Island.

Leave the boardwalk as you come to the first houses on Ward's and walk south on the quiet beach, from the tip of which you'll get a good view of the south shore of all the islands. Follow the informal paths through the beach dune and meadow wetland area east of the beachfront back toward the outer edge of Ward's. Follow the outer avenues around to the city side of the island and then to the Ward's Island ferry dock. In the off-season, the walk ends here. In season, if you want to continue, follow the north shore until you come to the large wooden bridge leading to Algonquin Island. The homes on Algonquin are somewhat larger than those on Ward's, and there is a nice wooded section on the western tip of the island.

Leave Algonquin by the same bridge and follow the main path west to the wooden bridge leading to Snake Island. There is a pleasant picnic area in the centre of Snake Island surrounded by dense stands of cottonwoods, so this could make a good lunch spot. Also, a path leads out to the island's north shore, from which you'll get a good view of the city.

Leaving Snake Island, turn right and follow the main path west through formal and busier parkland. Follow the signs for the Centre Island ferry docks. From these docks, there is frequent service back to the city. On public holidays and summer Sundays, however, you might be better to backtrack to the Ward's Island docks to avoid the Centre Island crowds.

Wilket Creek, Taylor Creek and Warden Woods

LENGTH: 10 kilometres
TIME: 4 hours
TERRAIN: Flat, except for an informal path in Warden Woods
DIRECTIONS: By car, drive to the Civic Garden Centre at the southwest corner of Lawrence Avenue East and Leslie Street. You'll have to get back to your car by transit. By transit, take the Lawrence 54 bus from the Eglinton subway station to the Civic Garden Centre. The walk ends at either Victoria Park or Warden subway station.

On any map of Toronto, the Don River and its tributaries make up a large network of green space in the heart of the city. For decades, however, destructive human activities have encroached on these green spaces. We've built expressways and rail lines, hydro corridors and sewers down the valleys. Roads, subdivisions and other developments have been built to the very top edges of the valley slopes. But this network of creeks, ravines and the branches of the Don itself remains a critical web of corridors for wildlife, and now plans abound for rehabilitating the Don and its tributaries. This walk along some of the Don's most important feeder streams should give walkers a good sense both of what's being done to "bring back the Don" and of the long road ahead.

Starting from the parking lot at the Civic Garden Centre, take the paved path south into the valley. At the first junction, turn left into Wilket Creek Park. There's little formal parkland left in this steep-sided valley. Aside from mown strips alongside the path, natural regeneration is the order. Right away you'll see cattails flourishing in low wet spots and an abundance of shrubs that provide both cover and berries for birds. Moving down the valley, the walker passes a number of substantial white pine trees, at least one of which looks as though it has been taken advantage of by a sapsucker searching for insects under its bark. The valley is well shaded and the creek is for the most part free to wander along the valley floor.

As you enter Sunnybrook Park, follow the signs near the washrooms pointing toward Victoria Park station. This means leaving the paved path that dead-ends at Leslie Street in favour of the roadway running south through the park. Follow the road, and with it the West Don, under Eglinton Avenue. At the end of the parking lot on the south side of Eglinton, the paved path resumes, working its way under the railway trestle and into Ernest Thompson Seton Park.

In the 1870s and '80s, Ernest Seton spent all the time he could exploring the natural life of the Don and its tributary valleys. His fascination with natural history and natural processes led Seton, a gold medal winner from the Ontario College of Art, to publish numerous books, including *Wild Animals I Have Known.* Unfortunately, Seton park itself now consists mostly of uninteresting expanses of mown turf.

Walk along the eastern edge of the grass where the more naturalized areas of the park are. There are informal paths you can follow into the naturalized areas, including one near a large wooden sign marking tree plantings which leads down to a small wetland. Take care in this area not to trample any vegetation or startle birds or other animals, and double back on the path you followed down.

Passing by the back door of the Ontario Science Centre, the path leads under Overlea Boulevard. Here there is a picnic shelter and, a little further south, washrooms. The path then leads toward the confluence of the branches of the Don—and a bit of a maze of overpasses, on-ramps and railway lines. Follow the signs for Victoria Park, crossing over the railway tracks on a footbridge, then the East Don on a small stone bridge and then under the Don Valley Parkway before entering Taylor Creek Park.

Leaving the parking lot at Taylor Creek Park, the walk starts angling more east than south. Here again, the valley is narrower and more naturalized with tall sumacs, grasses and ferns pushing up against the path. Taylor Creek apparently has had a number of different names over the years, including Silver Creek and Massey Creek (after the Massey family). And while the valley remains an important migration corridor for birds working their way from the east side of Toronto over to the Don, the character of the creek itself has been distinctly changed since the Masseys may have known it. It has been straightened and channelized for almost its entire length. As well, the last significant remnant of the tableland oak forests that fed water gradually down into the creek was destroyed for a residential development in the

1970s. A large sanitary sewer also now runs under the path alongside the straightened creek.

The valley still has wild characteristics, however. In summer the gabions that line the creek are covered in wild grape, nettles and nightshade, and bird species, such as the eastern wood pee wee, more usually associated with rural areas can often be seen here. The water quality of Taylor Creek, like that of the Don and Wilket Creek, suffers from the problems of most urban streams: contaminated run-off from roads and other asphalt areas, legal and illegal discharges of storm and sanitary sewers from both residential and industrial areas and, in some places, lack of cover, making the stream water too warm for cold-water lake species to spawn in. Also, because the stream is channelized, there is no way for these contaminants to be filtered out by plant materials, and water volumes and speeds can change abruptly, in ways that are deadly to aquatic life.

When you reach the end of Taylor Creek Park at Victoria Park Avenue, walk south and cross at the lights before continuing south to Victoria Park subway station. From here you can decide whether you want to continue your walk through Warden Woods to Warden station or pack it in for the day. If you're continuing, follow the walkway along the north side of the subway line until you come to an apartment complex. Follow the roadway out of the complex to Pharmacy Avenue. Cross Pharmacy and jog north to the road entrance to Warden Woods. Follow the road past the works yard to the beginning of the paved path through the woods. It's a pleasant 2.5-kilometre walk from here to Warden station through a valley that has, as well as the usual hardwood species, quite a number of large cedar and pine trees. In fact, in areas that are being allowed to regenerate, the plantings are dominated by evergreens, such as white and red pine and balsam fir.

For walkers who have been itching to get off the pavement, your chance comes a little ways into the valley

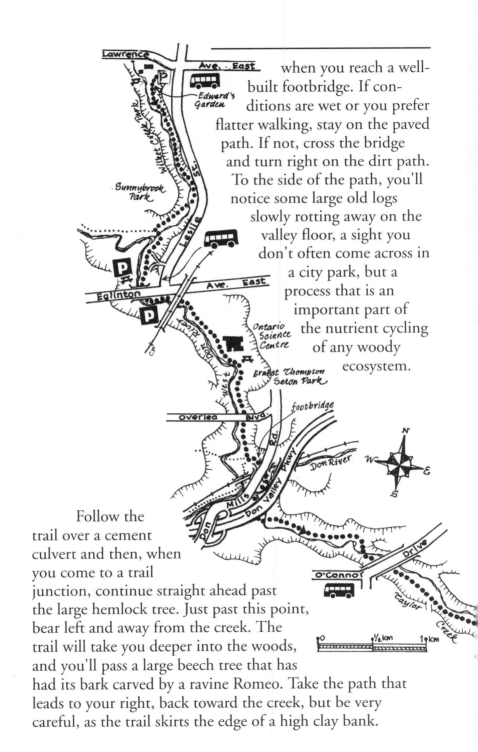

when you reach a well-built footbridge. If conditions are wet or you prefer flatter walking, stay on the paved path. If not, cross the bridge and turn right on the dirt path. To the side of the path, you'll notice some large old logs slowly rotting away on the valley floor, a sight you don't often come across in a city park, but a process that is an important part of the nutrient cycling of any woody ecosystem.

Follow the trail over a cement culvert and then, when you come to a trail junction, continue straight ahead past the large hemlock tree. Just past this point, bear left and away from the creek. The trail will take you deeper into the woods, and you'll pass a large beech tree that has had its bark carved by a ravine Romeo. Take the path that leads to your right, back toward the creek, but be very careful, as the trail skirts the edge of a high clay bank.

Follow the trail away from the creek again and then take the branch leading uphill on your right. The trail leads you up a steep slope through a maple-beech-oak forest, through a dip and then to a point where you can look out over the valley. From here, turn left and follow the trail along the side ravine until the path dips down to a small stream at a crossing point marked by boulders on the opposite bank. Cross here and follow the spine of the ridge down in the direction of the creek. When the ridge comes to a point, turn left and descend the steep slope. Follow the bottom of the slope around a small slough and, where the trail comes up to a thicket of raspberry canes, turn left and follow the trail to the top of the slope where you emerge onto the lawn of a school. Follow the valley edge through the schoolyard until you reach St. Clair Avenue, then walk east to Warden station.

   If you've followed the paved path, leave the valley via the stairs on your right.

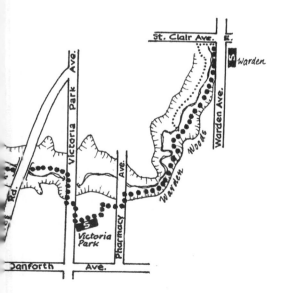

Darlington Provincial Park and McLaughlin Bay Wildlife Reserve

LENGTH: Darlington, 4 kilometres; *Darlington Prov. Park.*
McLaughlin Bay, 3.2 kilometres
TIME: 2 hours
TERRAIN: Trails are unblazed but well signed and easy to
follow. Trail surfaces are wood chip, crushed limestone or
mown grass. Easy walking.
DIRECTIONS: Take Highway 401 to exit 419 in Oshawa.
Drive south on Farewell Street to Colonel Sam Drive. Turn
left onto Colonel Sam Drive and continue past the General
Motors head office. On your left is the pedestrian entrance to
Darlington park; on your right, free parking for a few cars.

Expressways, apartment towers, high-priced housing estates,
oil refineries and other commercial uses have all helped to cut
off our urban centres from the lakefront. How many of us

even think of Toronto as a city on the water? To the east of
Toronto, however, the combination of Darlington Provincial
Park and the McLaughlin Bay Wildlife Reserve, owned by
General Motors, has kept a significant stretch of the Lake
Ontario shoreline in a more natural state, for the enjoyment
of both people and animals. By combining the trail systems
of the two areas, you can follow a pleasant figure-8 walk
through interesting meadows and along the lakeshore.

Enter Darlington Provincial Park by the pedestrian
entrance. Turn left immediately inside the gate and start
walking on the boundary trail. This section of trail is noisy,
thanks to the proximity of Highway 401, but it is cool and
shaded. After about a kilometre, the trail turns south, crosses
a park road and continues alongside a picnic area, where it is
signed as a fitness trail. At the next road crossing, turn left
and immediately turn left again to start on the nature trail
along Robinson Creek.

This is the most secluded section of trail in the park.
There are some big willows lining the creek and the footpath
is shaded by their branches. Watch for hummingbirds in the
orange jewelweed growing in the wet ground under the
willows. Near the beginning of this loop is a large patch of
purple asters—a good place to look for monarch butterflies
collecting nectar in the fall. There is also a lot of high-bush
cranberry along the creek, which is attractive both for its
flowers and its bright red berries. Toward late winter, those
berries will be looking attractive to cedar waxwings, which by
then will be unable to find any sweeter fruit.

At the end of the nature trail, cross the road and continue south along Robinson Creek to Lake Ontario. Turn
right and follow the trail along the lakeshore past the Darlington Pioneer Home, a log house restored by the township
of Darlington as a centennial project. Walk past the boat
rental and continue west along the shore of McLaughlin Bay.
The beach along this stretch is well known to birders as a
good place to watch shorebirds and gulls. Sharp-tailed

sparrows are also often seen along the marshy edges during migration.

The mown-grass trail you are following ends at a parking lot. Continue from here, alongside the gravel road that leads to it, back to the pedestrian entrance. Leave the park by the entrance and turn right onto the road. On your left you will see a trail leading toward the General Motors head office and a map of the McLaughlin Bay Wildlife Reserve.

The reserve consists of 267 hectares (108 acres) of prime waterfront land. The property was formerly a dairy farm, but General Motors has committed itself to transforming the area into a diverse natural habitat area open to the public for passive recreational use. The long-term plan is to transform parts of the property into various forest and shrub-thicket zones to provide habitat and migration corridors for birds and other mammals. Already, more than 250 species of birds and 22 species of mammals have been identified on the reserve, and the hope is that, by providing food and cover, the numbers of both resident and migrant species will be increased.

Follow the paved trail marked on the map board to the highest point on the reserve. A number of maple trees have been planted at the top of the hill, and picnic tables and a bird feeding station help to create a pleasant rest stop. From the hilltop, you also get a good view of the entire reserve. To the east is McLaughlin Bay and Darlington park; to the west, Second Marsh, at the mouths of Harmony and Farewell creeks.

A quick walk through the reserve yielded sightings of a marsh hawk, a flock of cedar waxwings, a belted kingfisher, a great blue heron, a savannah sparrow, two pairs of common loons, many goldfinches (eating thistle seeds), Canada geese and two double-crested cormorants. Bring binoculars and you'll be able to see a number of ducks and mergansers.

For nonbirders, the reserve is still a picturesque meadow with fine views of the lake. To see the rest of the property, walk back down from the top of the hill and take the first trail on your right, following it as it loops in a clockwise direction. To extend your walk, continue along the berm on the east side of Second Marsh until you reach a pumping station. Return by the same route to the General Motors headquarters building and from there to your car.

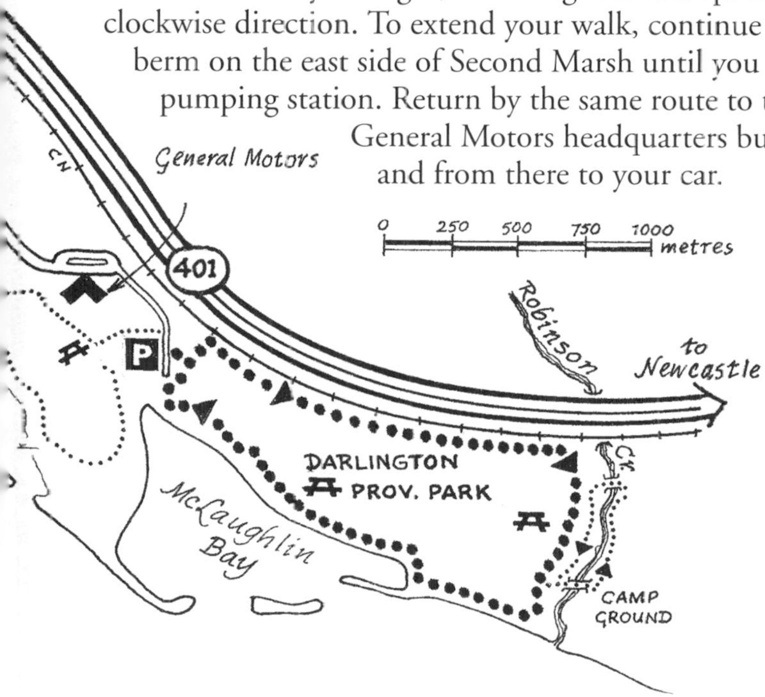

General Motors

0 250 500 750 1000 metres

Robinson

to Newcastle

401

P

DARLINGTON PROV. PARK

McLaughlin Bay

Cr.

CAMP GROUND

Long Sault
Conservation Area

ruine
stone house
Long Sault C.A.

LENGTH: 8 kilometres
TIME: 2 ¹/₂ hours
TERRAIN: Rolling hills, with a couple of steep climbs.
Trails are generally wide and well marked.
DIRECTIONS: From Highway 401 eastbound, take the
first exit for Bowmanville (Waverly Road/Regional Road 57).
Follow 57 north to Concession 9 and turn right. The
conservation area is on the north side of the concession,
about two kilometres to the east of the intersection. Park in
the north lot. There are outhouses and picnic tables near the
parking lot. There is also a large chalet nearby, but it is
usually only open on weekends.

The Long Sault Conservation Area encompasses some of the
Oak Ridges Moraine's best features for walking—rolling
hills, pleasant viewpoints and shady forests. It also, however,
includes an example of one of the problems facing this long
strand of glacial till that runs from the Niagara Escarpment

to east of the Ganaraska River—gravel extraction. At the centre of the Long Sault property is a working gravel pit, which for walkers remains unseen but, depending on the day, may be heard.

The problem with digging gravel out of what is, after all, virtually a enormous mound of sand, rock and gravel is the possible effect on the many streams that are fed by the deep aquifers in the moraine. If the flow of these streams is interrupted or lowered, then downstream habitat, which includes almost the entire Greater Toronto Area, will be damaged. For example, along the steeper eastern sections of the moraine where Long Sault is located, fast, cold streams running down the moraine's south slope support a healthy trout fishery. If the level of these streams drops, the water becomes warmer and the trout can no longer survive.

The trailhead for the ski loops that double as hiking trails at Long Sault is located directly beside the north parking lot. Follow the main access trail along the edge of a small stream and through a stand of young poplars until you come to the first trail junction. Turn left here and follow the black trail through a gap in the fence and out into an area of open, rolling fields. This area should be particularly pretty in the fall, thanks to both the asters and goldenrod in the fields and to the views of the surrounding woods. As you ramble up and down the small hillocks, you'll also get a sense of the interesting topography of the moraine. Take your time and watch to see if any birds are using the man-made bluebird boxes scattered through here, or watch for butterflies visiting the wildflowers.

The trail takes to the edge of the open field to follow a narrow ridge line dotted with birches and pine trees for a short stretch and then heads back out onto open ground. When the trail reaches the shell of an old stone building, it turns right and descends toward a hardwood bush.

Follow the trail straight into this shady forest and then veer left with it into the more southerly end of the forest.

The trail section through here is low-lying and wet; cedar and hemlock begin to predominate, rather than the hardwoods such as birch and maple that surrounded the entrance to the woods.

The trail crosses a bridge over a small creek and continues to wind through the woods before it makes a sharp left and leads up a steep hill, through a pine plantation. Pines have always been at home on the drier, sandier sections of the moraine, and reforestation efforts begun in the 1930s to combat erosion of the moraine's unstable soils caused by farm clearances have often relied on the planting of thousands of these conifers, including both red and white pine. In fact, the moraine is often still referred to as the Great Pine Ridge.

At the top of the hill, the trail continues through the pines, crossing straight over an access road. On the other side of the road, the trail shortly emerges from the woods to skirt an open field and then runs downhill through another section of pine. The trail makes a few more turns through the pines and then enters a mature hardwood forest.

The trail climbs regularly in this next section, following a narrow ridge through a mixed deciduous forest. The canopy is thick through here and the trail is sun-dappled and relatively narrow.

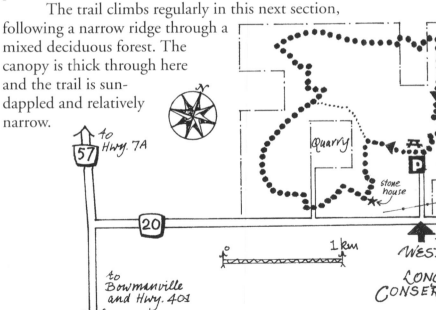

N

57 to Hwy. 7A

Quarry

stone house

20

to Bowmanville and Hwy. 401

1 km

WEST

LONG CONSER

102

The trail eventually reaches a high point of land, but only when the leaves are off the trees will you get much of a view. From this point, the trail turns right and heads straight toward a block of pine. It follows the edge of these pines for a while before turning in and running downhill through an area of mixed pine and deciduous forest. Shortly after, the walker reaches another trail junction. Turn left and continue to follow the markers for the black trail.

After the junction, the trail runs along the edge of the conservation authority property and beside a neighbouring farm. A number of large pines lean over the trail on the conservation area side, but shortly the trail swings east again and climbs uphill into an area of deciduous forest. The trail doesn't stay in the forest for long, however. It soon exits into an area of old field with scattered pines and lots of sumac. The trail then makes a couple of turns through this open area before heading back into the deciduous forest.

From here on, the trail crosses flatter terrain, so the section ahead shouldn't take long to finish. After passing through a section of pines, the trail makes a few dips through a stand of maples and oaks before coming out to a young conifer plantation. The trail circles around the plantation on a flat, open track before finally cutting through an open field at the plantation's south end and returning to the starting point.

For those who would rather not follow this last section, at the point where the black trail makes a sharp turn to the left after reentering the hardwood bush, it's possible to cross to the blue trail, which runs virtually parallel at this point. The blue trail will quickly take you back to the parking lot through the rolling heart of the woodlot.

to Hwy. 35

EAST

AREAS

Long Sault Conservation Area – East

Black trail sign
Long Sault C.A

LENGTH: 4.3 kilometres

TIME: 1 ¹/₂ hours

TERRAIN: Rolling hills, with a couple of short, steep climbs. The trail is well marked.

DIRECTIONS: Continue 1 kilometre east from the main entrance to the Long Sault Conservation Area on Concession 9. The entrance to the east section is not marked from the concession; look for an entrance road on the north side surrounded by evergreens.

This loop covers similar terrain to the trails in the conservation area's western part but seems to be less well used. If you have the energy, it can make a nice addition to the walk described for the main area and, with less human traffic, your chances of seeing deer and other animals over here is definitely increased.

The trail starts off from the gate at the east end of the parking lot and quickly branches right at a marked junction. It passes through an area with heavy thickets hung with lots of berries, which should make this an attractive corridor for birds. Also along the way are a number of old fruit trees.

Emerging from this narrow corridor, the trail stays in the open, running along the base of some small hills and then along the bottom of a heavily wooded ridge.

The trail continues to climb toward the north end of the property and makes a steep climb through a pretty woods with lots of white birch. After crossing through an open field at the top that is in the process of being retaken by poplar and aspen saplings, the trail descends a gentle hill to the base of a large deciduous woods. There is a steep climb to gain entry to this stately forest, which changes from a mixture of birch and pine at its southern edge to a mix of beech, hemlock and maple in the interior. It's cool, shady walking through the woods as the trail continues north and then bends west, eventually completing a 180-degree turn.

Leaving the woods at the southern edge, the trail skirts a field planted with conifer seedlings and then tracks along the edge of a more mature planting of spruce and pine. To the south of this block of trees, the trail crosses through an open hilly area under some hydro lines, offering walkers a good view of the moraine landscape, before descending a long hill back to the trail junction. Turning right at this junction brings you back to the parking lot.

See map on pages 102–3.

Lynde Shores
Conservation Area

LENGTH: 2 kilometres
TIME: 1 hour
TERRAIN: Flat. Along the creek, the trail may have wet sections.
DIRECTIONS: From Highway 401, take Highway 12 south to Regional Road 22 (Victoria Street). Head west on 22 until you see the conservation area parking lot on your left.

Timing may be everything when visiting Lynde Shores. The prime attraction of this extensive marsh area is the birds that nest here or stop over during spring and fall migrations. Bring your binoculars and be prepared to move slowly and carefully, keeping a constant eye out for such Lynde Shores regulars as black ducks, blue wing teals, great blue herons and green herons, great horned owls, marsh hawks and yellow-shafted flickers. The conservation authority organizes staff-assisted waterfowl viewing days in spring and fall; call (416) 579-0411 for dates and times.

From the northeast corner of the parking lot, take a stroll out on the short boardwalk to get a good look at Lynde Creek and Storey Marsh. Returning to the parking lot, follow the gravel road south across the bridge until you see the start of the bird-feeder trail on your right. This is a short loop through a pleasant hardwood forest of maple, birch and hemlock. There are close to two dozen feeding stations set up along the trail and, if you're lucky, you'll spot something other than a raiding squirrel perched on a feeder.

From the end of the bird-feeder trail, walk back up the road until you see a path leading off to the right just before the bridge (directly opposite the starting point of the feeder trail). This is the start of a informal trail that follows Lynde Creek for more than a kilometre. It starts off through an area of alder thickets and solitary northern pin oaks. At almost any point along this path, there are good views of the creek.

The path actually cuts through a narrow treed band, with the creek on one side and open fields on the other. As you work your way south, you pass in and out of pockets of oak trees, some more mature than others. At times, the path breaks completely into the open, cutting through shrubby sections that are good places to look for songbirds.

Passing into a final set of oak woods, this time with a thick understorey of vines, the walker reaches the edge of a marshy inlet. From here, looking south, you can see the lake breaking against the beach at the mouth of the creek, but the inlet cuts off any possibility of continuing further south. From the southern edge of the woods,

Along the bird feeder trail

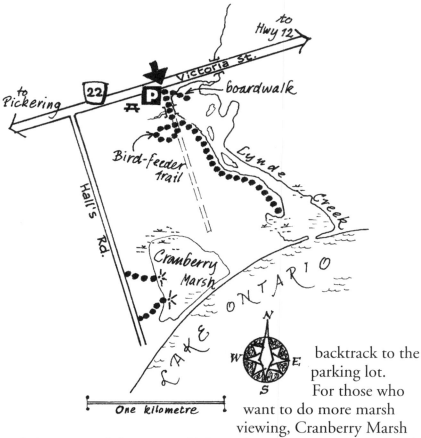

backtrack to the parking lot.

For those who want to do more marsh viewing, Cranberry Marsh is just around the corner. Drive a short way west on Regional Road 22 (Victoria Street) and turn left at the first side road you come to (Hall's Road). About a kilometre down this road, you will come to the first of two paths that lead out to platforms that offer sweeping views of the marsh. From the more northerly platform, you can see an osprey nest located at the top end of the marsh.

Rouge Marshes

Rouge River Marshes with chimney

LENGTH: 3 kilometres

TIME: 1 ¹/₂ hours

TERRAIN: This is not a difficult trail, but it can be wet and somewhat overgrown, so sturdy footwear and long-sleeved shirts and long pants are recommended.

DIRECTIONS: By transit, take the Rouge Hill 13 bus from the Rouge Hill GO station. This is a limited service route, so call (416)393-INFO for schedule information before you go. Get off at the corner of Rouge Hills Drive and Island Road. By car, take Highway 401 to Port Union Road and Port Union Road south to Island Road. There is no parking on Island Road, so you will have to leave your car on Rouge Hills Drive and walk down Island Road to the starting point.

Exploring the bottom lands and marshes of the lower Rouge, this route has quite a different feel to it than does the walk described for the Rouge tablelands. Down here, vine-draped trees, dense thickets and abundant ostrich-fern groves create almost a feeling of being somewhere in the Deep South. Of course, upper slopes studded with sugar maple, red oak, red maple and white pine help to remind walkers that they are still somewhere north of Lake Ontario.

Starting from the road barrier at the end of Island Road, follow the well-worn path down toward the valley bottom. But instead of following the path right to the banks of the river, take the first path branching off to the left. This path follows the bottom of a slope dominated by red oak and sugar maple. The path continues to angle toward the river and skirts around some small oxbows—the remains of old meanders. As the path settles on a route through the bottom land forest of Manitoba maple and crack willow, you will pass a hardwood-forested terrace on your left. The difference in plant communities between the bottom lands and this only slightly higher terrace can probably be explained by the fact that the terrace is just high enough to avoid the yearly flooding endured by the trees below. In fact, if you're doing this walk in the early spring, you may find yourself walking on a thick layer of silt deposited by the spring floods.

After a short walk, the trail ascends at a point where the valley slope pinches in against the river, leaving no way round. There are a number of large hemlock trees here, and you can get a bit of a view of the valley from about the halfway point of the hill, but don't follow the path all the way to the top; it leads into a private yard.

Instead, turn back and follow the path along the river bank south. The river is much wider and murkier now that all the tributaries have consolidated for the final push to the lake. There is still enough flow, however, for bank edges to be steadily eaten away, so step carefully along those stretches where the trail follows the very edge of the bank.

On more than one occasion, the path has to pull back from the river to get around obstacles such as fallen trees or impenetrable masses of river-grape vines. Along this section you'll find long pants and a long-sleeved shirt especially handy, as many branches and vines overhang the trail.

Just before reaching the junction with the path leading back to Island Road, the trail skirts around the remains of an old snag. Only the bottom half of this long-dead tree is still standing, and it is clear from the holes, large and small, that cover it that it's well on its way to being returned to the soil.

Continue following the river south past the T junction and you'll notice an old stone chimney standing on the opposite bank. This section of the Rouge Valley was, in fact, a well-developed cottaging area for Toronto residents until Hurricane Hazel swept the community away in 1954.

Passing a meander that has created a sheer sand cliff on the opposite bank, you are now closing in on the Rouge marshes. There's a small stream to jump over, and then in another hundred metres, you'll find yourself standing at the northern edge of the marshes.

The Rouge is one of the few rivers in the Toronto area whose marshes have remained pretty much undisturbed, and this is the place to bring out the binoculars and look for birds, whether migrating songbirds sheltering in the dogwood thickets that ring the blue-joint grass meadows nearby or water birds such as herons or terns nesting in the wet meadows and marshes to the south.

When you're ready to turn back, follow the path back to the major T junction and turn left, following the path back to Island Road. But before you leave, take a short walk along the beautiful ridge that extends south from the roadway. Pick up the trail at the end of the green wooden barrier on the south side of Island Road and follow it as it wanders through a forest of sugar maple, red oak, red maple, white pine and hemlock. Some of the trees growing on this ridge are obviously well over a hundred years old, judging from their size, and after the humidity of the valley, the cool shade of the ridge makes quite a contrast.

Near some large hemlocks, the trail offers a great vista of the top end of the marshes before descending steeply to follow the bank above a marsh inlet. Passing through an open stand of white birches, the trail turns back upriver and cuts through the bottom lands, eventually reaching a junction with another well-used path. Turn left at this junction and follow the path past an area of dogwoods and sumacs in the direction of a solitary white pine tree. The trail shortly begins to climb, bringing you back to the road barrier at Island Road.

See map on page 114–15.

Rouge River and Little Rouge Creek

Rouge River   Highway 2 overpass

LENGTH: 10 kilometres

TIME: 2 hours

TERRAIN: Rolling hills, with one steep climb in the first half; flat for the second half

DIRECTIONS: Take Meadowvale Road north from Highway 401 to Sheppard Avenue. Turn east on Sheppard and continue east on Twyn Rivers Drive. When Sheppard swings south, park in the large lot at the abandoned ski hill (on your right after the second bridge). By the TTC, take the Scarboro 86 bus from the Kennedy station or the Sheppard East 85 bus from the Sheppard station to the corner of Sheppard and Meadowvale. It's a 1-kilometre walk from the bus stop to the starting point of the trail.

Nowhere else within the boundaries of Metro Toronto will a walker feel as surrounded by nature as along the Rouge. Walking along a ridge line under the shade of maples and beech trees, it's easy to forget about the city and its expressways.

112

A lunch spot could be a gravel bar on a meander of the Rouge or one of its tributaries.

There is, however, plenty of traffic in the Rouge. The valley is used by walkers out to stretch pavement-weary legs, bicyclists tired of dodging car doors and horse riders who come in from nearby stables. The valleys and tablelands are also used as shelter and travel corridors by a small herd of white-tailed deer and by foxes, raccoons and other small mammals, as well. For migratory birds, the Rouge Valley is a natural flyway and rest spot.

At more than 4,500 hectares, the Rouge offers room for all these uses and, in fact, will shortly become Canada's largest urban park. The Rouge lands avoided the development fate of Toronto's other river systems, such as the Don and the Humber, when the provincial government designated the area a greenbelt for its proposed Pickering airport in the 1970s. In 1990, after much debate, the Rouge lands, still in a mostly natural state, were finally designated to become a national park.

One of the best areas for walking in the Rouge is on the tableland separating the Rouge River and the Little Rouge Creek just above their confluence. The trail actually starts at the southern end of the Little Rouge Bridge. (The footbridge from the ski hill parking lot across the Little Rouge has been washed out.) Follow the trail along the Little Rouge back to the ski hill and start climbing—but take a few pauses to admire the view. The open field of the old ski hill is home to lots of bird life, and at the top, maple and poplar saplings have started to take back the slope.

Informal trails crisscross the Rouge, but even if you wander off on a side trail, it's fairly easy to reorient yourself by studying the direction of the river or the ridge. At worst, you'll soon pass a road or highway overpass that will tell you exactly where you are.

At the top of the ski hill, turn left (south) and enjoy the shade of the thick deciduous forest around you. One of

the most interesting things about the Rouge is the stark
differences between the north and south slopes of
the river valleys. The warm, dry, south-facing
slopes are populated by sun-loving and drought-
resistant trees such as oak and pine. In places,
the Rouge's southern slopes also support uncommon, warmth-loving Carolinian plants such
as the dry-land blueberry. On the colder, wetter
north slopes, you'll see hemlock and sugar maple,
trees most often found further north. These plant
communities present dramatic evidence of the microclimates
that exist within the larger climate of Southern Ontario.

As you continue south along the ridge, the canopy
opens up and sunlight streams in between tall white pines.
The trail is a bit more rolling along this narrow ridge section,
but it remains relatively smooth and well trodden. At the
bottom of a dip, trails break off to the left and right, but
head straight through, following the ridge. At the southern
tip of the trail you are following, there are good views of the
Rouge River Valley. Don't head down the steep gully the trail
descends at this point, however. Instead, double back to the
first major trail branching off to your right. This is a wide
trail that cuts through a stand of hemlock, then quickly
comes to a T junction, at which you turn right. The trail
you're now on will wind you right down to the bank of the
Little Rouge Creek. Careful, it can get muddy and slick on
the downhill run.

At the creek, turn right and follow the trail until you
see a campground across the Rouge River, which is on your
right. (If you come to the highway overpass you've gone too
far.) From here, pick up the trail that follows the bank of the
Rouge across from the campground and start walking upriver. (The Glenn Rouge Campground and its facilities are
off-limits to everyone except campers.)

The walk along the river is flat and easy and, except
for the willows and cedars along the banks, takes you past

114

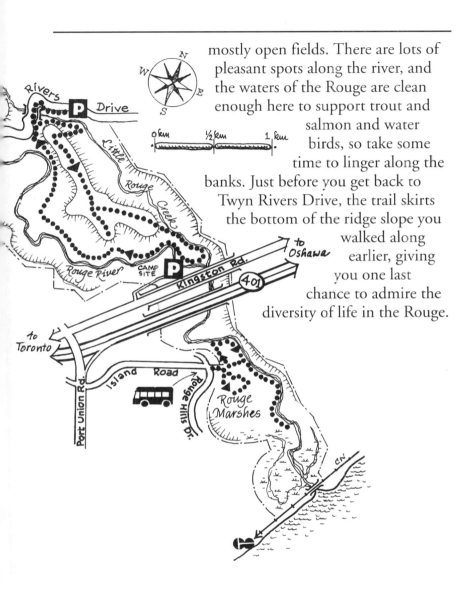

mostly open fields. There are lots of pleasant spots along the river, and the waters of the Rouge are clean enough here to support trout and salmon and water birds, so take some time to linger along the banks. Just before you get back to Twyn Rivers Drive, the trail skirts the bottom of the ridge slope you walked along earlier, giving you one last chance to admire the diversity of life in the Rouge.

Bennett Heritage Trail and the Silver Creek Loop

Scotsdale Farm

LENGTH: Approximately 13 kilometres
TIME: 4 1/2 hours
TERRAIN: No steep ascents, but quite a bit of walking up and down hills and many stiles (fence ladders). Some rough footing, especially on limestone.
DIRECTIONS: Enter Scotsdale Farm (open daily nine a.m. to five p.m.) from Trafalgar Road just north of Highway 7. The sign is set back from the road. Look for it soon after you cross 27 Side Road. Drive toward the main farmhouse and park near the sign for the Bennett Heritage Trail. Access is free.

This is a walk to take your time on. There are a variety of things to see and explore, and the distance is long enough that you'll want to take some rest and snack breaks. The Bennett Heritage Trail is quite new; it officially opened on Canada Day 1992. The trail explores Scotsdale Farm, which was donated to the Ontario Heritage Foundation in 1982 by

Stewart and Violet Bennett. The 1,300-hectare property abuts the Niagara Escarpment, and in addition to the rather special ecological qualities that this proximity gives to the farm, it is also an interesting historical site. The farm has actually been worked for more than two centuries, having been tilled by native people before the arrival of Europeans. The farm remains a working farm, so please keep dogs on a leash! The property is managed by the Credit Valley Conservation Authority.

Beginning at the sign for the Bennett Heritage Trail, walk southwest, in the direction of Trafalgar Road, along a farm lane bordered by Norway spruce. The trail is marked with blue blazes. The trail leads from the lane into a mature woodlot of maple, beech and handsome white pines. Just before you reach Trafalgar Road, the trail swings left over a cedar-rail fence. At this point, you will see a trail map on your right. Head left on the Bruce Trail (white blazes) and enter the woods.

The trail meanders through the woods and several pastures before emerging at the 8th Line. There are cows using these pastures so watch out for patties and don't let Rover off his leash. At the 8th Line, cross the road and turn right and walk past a small wetland on your right. At the double white blaze, turn left and enter the woods. Here the trail runs over limestone erratics (chunks of limestone left behind by glaciers), so watch your step. This is a quite picturesque section of the trail, and the woods here are full of interesting ferns.

When the blue blazes begin again, follow them to the right. This is the Silver Creek Loop. It can be muddy through this section, and side trails can be misleading; follow the blue blazes. At the bottom of the loop, you will come to a hickory tree with two blue and two yellow blazes. (We saw a black-billed cuckoo here.) The options at this point are to continue on the blue trail or to explore the 2-kilometre yellow loop. The yellow loop leads to an old mill site and pond before returning to the hickory tree. Crossing Highway 7 interrupts the rural charm of the walk, however, and the loop is not well marked.

If you decide to continue on the blue trail, go left at the marked hickory tree and follow the blue blazes through a meadow before entering a forest of mature hemlock, maple and white birch. You will follow a wooded ridge before going over a stile and rejoining the main Bruce Trail (white blazes). Make a right onto the main trail and follow it across the 8th Line and into the woods. Snow's Creek runs along on your right. Soon, you'll reach a pretty spot where the trail crosses the creek on a wooden bridge.

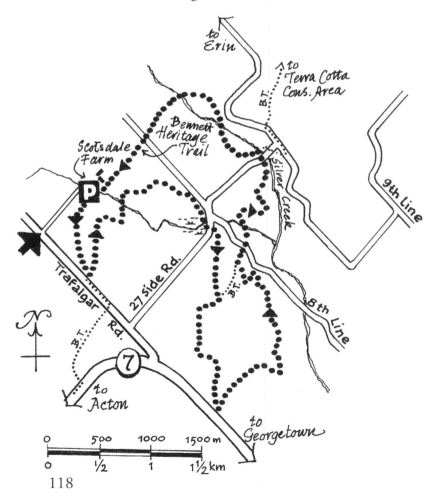

After this, the trail crosses a short boardwalk, climbs a set of log stairs and then bends to the right through some mature hemlocks. Pay attention to the blazes on this section, as another well-travelled trail goes off to the right just before you reach 27 Side Road.

At 27 Side Road, those who want to add distance—and a bit of a challenge—to this walk can turn right here and continue to follow the white blazes of the Bruce Trail a kilometre north to the Silver Creek Overlook Side Trail, marked with blue blazes. This rugged path takes hikers to the top of the escarpment by way of a narrow cleft between two rock walls and, finally, a ladder to an overlook spot. From here, the side trail descends to rejoin the main trail. Turn left on the main trail, and it will bring you back to the junction you left from. Those who do not want to add this somewhat challenging loop to their walk should stop following the white blazes once they reach 27 Side Road. Instead, cross the road, and a few steps to your left, you will find a stile, a map and the start of the Bennett Heritage Trail (blue blazes).

Follow the blue blazes along the fence line, through the woods, over the creek onto the farm lane and across the 8th Line back to the farm buildings where you began your hike. These farm buildings were built by caring hands and are well worth a careful look. The stone walls around the farmhouse in particular are a marvel. Behind the house, there is a pond created by a dam across Snow's Creek. On our walk, we saw mute swans and a belted kingfisher there.

Borer's Falls and Rock Chapel Sanctuary

Borer's Falls

LENGTH: Approximately 6 kilometres
TIME: 4 hours (including Armstrong Trail side trip)
TERRAIN: York Road to Borer's Falls: hilly with one steep ascent. Rock Chapel loop: flat. Armstrong Trail: steep. Trails are generally well-maintained dirt paths; Royal Botanical Gardens (RBG) trails are somewhat wider and flatter.
DIRECTIONS: From Highway 403 take Highway 6 north to York Road. Take York Road west and park in the lot marked North Shore Trails, RBG.

This walk, thanks to both the workings of nature and the work of the Royal Botanical Gardens' staff in explaining the former, is rich in features. It also brings us in close contact with the Niagara Escarpment, the physical feature that prominantly defines the western edge of the Greater Toronto Area. The escarpment is a shale and limestone ridge, gouged out by glaciers more than twelve thousand years ago, that runs from the Niagara River in the south to the tip of the Bruce Peninsula in the north. Water percolates through the layers of glacial till and porous limestone of the escarpment, often bubbling through the loose rock talus at the bottom of the slope as clear springs.

The escarpment has an ecology all its own. The thin soil of the windswept plateau above tends to stunt the tree and plant growth on the top of the ridge. It has recently been discovered, for example, that some small, gnarled cedars on the cliff edge are as much as eight hundred years old. (See the display to the left of the Rock Chapel parking lot.) On the escarpment face, mosses and lichens gain a tenuous toehold, while tree seedlings try to take advantage of any soil-covered ledges or fissures filled with plant detritus and the thinnest layer of mineral soil. The moisture that seeps out through the broken rock that has fallen to the bottom of the escarpment, known as the talus slope, by contrast supports an area of dense, thriving vegetation.

The escarpment also marks a watershed boundary (or divide); it is the westernmost source for waters flowing into Lake Ontario.

From the parking lot off York Road, cross the road, following the blue blazes that indicate a Bruce Trail side trail. At the double blue blaze (double blazes indicate a change in direction), turn toward the escarpment and enter a wooded area managed by the Hamilton Region Conservation Authority. There are very picturesque views along here, especially where Borer's Creek crosses the trail. The blue trail is well marked. Stick to it and do not be misled by other informal trails. The side trail ends when it meets the main Bruce Trail (white blazes). Turn left (south) onto the Bruce Trail and follow it up a steep ascent and then along the top of the

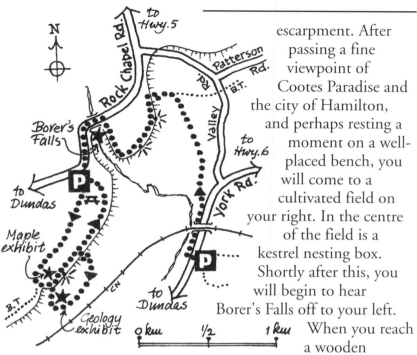

escarpment. After passing a fine viewpoint of Cootes Paradise and the city of Hamilton, and perhaps resting a moment on a well-placed bench, you will come to a cultivated field on your right. In the centre of the field is a kestrel nesting box. Shortly after this, you will begin to hear Borer's Falls off to your left. When you reach a wooden barricade placed between two stone pillars, you will have also reached the best vantage point for admiring the falls.

The power of this creek was used by the Borer family for more than a century to run a sawmill. However, by the early 1900s, land clearing had so altered the water flow of the creek that the mill had to convert to steam power.

Just above the falls, Rock Chapel Road crosses Borer's Creek. When you reach the road, turn left and follow it in the direction indicated by both an RBG sign and the Bruce Trail's white blazes. You will soon enter Rock Chapel Sanctuary where you might want to stop at the picnic tables for lunch. There is a map of the sanctuary to the right of the parking lot. Follow the mown RBG trail through the meadow to the RBG's Plant Succession Exhibit. This field demonstrates how natural processes take back an abandoned man-made clearing. The exhibit also includes information on plants and animals you're likely to see on this walk.

Continue on the RBG trail into a shady maple-oak forest. You will soon connect with the escarpment trail, where you will once again see the Bruce Trail's white blazes. Turn left and walk to the stone maple-sugar shack, which contains an extensive syrup-making display and a working evaporator. Every year, the RBG staff taps approximately 150 trees in this sugar bush and, if you're here in March, you can take advantage of an inexpensive pancake breakfast—served with fresh maple syrup of course—every Saturday and Sunday from ten a.m. to three p.m.

Just past the sugar shack on your right is another fine view of Hamilton, its harbour and the Burlington Skyway. Soon you will reach the junction of the escarpment trail, the Armstrong Trail (RBG) and another Bruce Trail side trail (blue blazes). These two side trails leave the escarpment trail together but quickly split. The blue trail goes left to a primitive campsite with good birding en route (look for house wrens, downy woodpeckers, hermit thrushes and brown creepers), while the Armstrong Trail goes right—and keeps right; do not be tempted to follow any trails going off to the left, as they only lead to private homes.

The Armstrong Trail brings you to an excellent geology display. In 1992, the display was in the process of being rebuilt. When it reopens, the display will allow you to get a close look at all the different layers, or strata, that make up the escarpment and will explain how each layer was created under ancient seas and mile-thick glaciers. After you're finished with the display, return back on the side trail to the main trail (white blazes) and follow it back to Borer's Falls. From the falls, take the blue trail back to your car.

Kestrel nesting box near Borer's Falls

123

Bronte Creek
Provincial Park – West Side

Bronte Stables ever hiehen

LENGTH: 7 kilometres
TIME: 2 ¹/₂ hours
TERRAIN: Mostly level with stairs leading down to the creek on Half Moon Valley Trail
DIRECTIONS: From the QEW take Burloak Drive north (between Oakville and Burlington). Enter the park from Burloak Drive and park in lot F. At the moment, there is no transit service to the park. There is a small day-use fee.

Bronte Creek is a well-developed recreational park. The trail system consists of three loops, and walkers can do one or all of them. (These trails are also open for cross-country skiing in winter.) The trails are generally wide with a hard-packed gravel surface, making them suitable for wheelchairs or strollers. The park also offers picnic sites and shelters, a food concession, a visitor's centre, baseball diamonds and tennis courts and a large swimming pool.

Before heading to the pool with your hot dog, however, explore the deep valley carved through beds of soft shale by Bronte Creek. From parking lot F, walk northeast

124

toward the working heritage farm. Enter the farmhouse at Spruce Lane Farm by the front door and take a guided tour of the house. Leave by the back door and walk through the farmyard. Behind the implement shed is the starting point of the well-named Trillium Trail. Unfortunately, this loop passes close to the QEW, so traffic noise is fairly constant, but in the springtime the beauty of a sugar bush carpeted with trilliums more than compensates.

On finishing the Trillium Trail loop turn right and connect to the Half Moon Valley Trail. (Guidebooks for this trail are available under the trail map sign.) Follow the Half Moon Trail to the right and down the stairs into the valley. This is a good place to watch for birds such as cardinals, goldfinches, house wrens and catbirds. Bronte Creek itself once served as a power source for early mills and factories in the area. Today, the creek is still clear enough to support a good variety of fish, including cohoe and chinook salmon, rainbow and brook trout and smallmouth bass. The trail will guide you through an interesting and sensitive wetland area before heading back up the stairs and out of the valley.

Turn right at the top and follow the trail to a lookout point with fine views of the valley. Notice the difference between the mostly coniferous north-facing slopes and the mostly deciduous south-facing slopes—a result of the microclimates created by the steep valley walls.

Upon leaving the Half Moon Valley Trail, turn right onto the gravel road; there is a pasture on your left as you walk along. Follow the gravel road around a turn to the left and then make an immediate right and follow the signs for the scenic lookout. At the end of the gravel road, enter the woods and walk along the Ravine Trail until you reach the lookout. This trail

pump activated by windmill

125

passes through a mature forest of hemlock, beech, ironwood and birch that has a distinctly "cathedral" feel to it.

From the lookout, leave the Ravine Trail and turn left. When you reach another gravel road, turn left again. Follow this laneway past an apple and pear orchard and a grapery. At the next junction, turn left again onto the Logging Trail. This trail passes through a woodlot with interpretative signs explaining the various experimental forestry techniques being used to manage the woodlot. The Logging Trail loops back to the laneway, where you'll see a sign once again for the scenic lookout. From here, you can follow the laneway back to Spruce Lane Farm and your car.

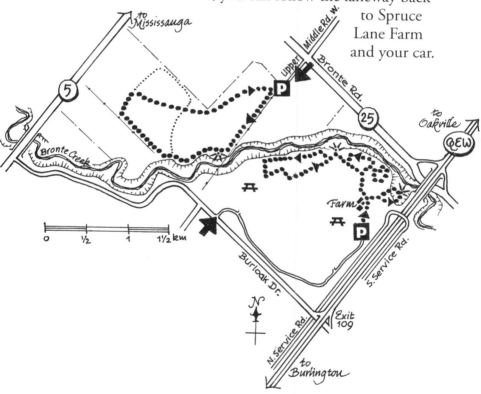

Bronte Creek
Provincial Park – East Side

Bronte

42 steps at No. 3

LENGTH: Approximately 4 kilometres
TIME: 1 $^1/_2$ hours
TERRAIN: Flat
DIRECTIONS: Turn west off Bronte Road (Highway 25) onto Upper Middle Road West. Park alongside the road where it dead-ends.

For those looking for something a little different from the full-service offerings of the west side of Bronte Creek park, the east side offers a chance to wander without distraction. (There are no facilities on this side of the park.) The paths on this side of the creek are informal—mostly horse trails, which can be quite slippery and mucky when wet. The path along the top of the ravine runs through a shady wood of aspens and oaks and offers good views of the creek below. This could be a great place to enjoy the fall colours, and it's a good place to look for woodland plant species such as trilliums or Indian pipe.

A suggested route: From the road, walk west along the hydro line through open fields and woods to the path running along the top of the ravine. Turn right and continue walking until you come to a telephone line overhead. Turn right again and follow the telephone line until you reach a well-worn horse track leading off to your right into a meadow. Follow this track through the meadow, staying to the right, back to the woodlot. Follow the trail along the edge of a cultivated field back to your car.

See map on page 126.

Crawford Lake and Rattlesnake Point

cuerthillevs

Crawford Lake - Indian Village Site

LENGTH: 10 kilometres

TIME: 4 ¹/₂ hours

TERRAIN: Rolling hills, with two steep ascents. Wear sturdy footwear.

DIRECTIONS: Take Guelph Line south from Highway 401 or north from the QEW and turn east at Steeles Avenue. There is a small day-use fee. Crawford Lake has an "all-terrain wheelchair program" involving lightweight, easy to push wheelchairs that can be borrowed for use on all the park's trails. The Crawford Lake Conservation Centre also features displays and activities, a theatre and a resource library, an indoor lunchroom and washrooms.

This route can introduce walkers to a bit of both the natural and the human history of Southern Ontario. The Crawford Lake Conservation Area features a historically accurate recreation of a fifteenth-century Iroquoian village (meaning its inhabitants belonged to the Iroquoian language group); the reconstruction has been based on actual archaeological evidence retrieved on the site. The village features two complete longhouses and several others in various stages of construction and demonstrations of village organization and village life, as well.

The proximity of the Niagara Escarpment adds much to the element of natural beauty and history. This walk traverses the Nassagaweya Canyon, a steep-sided chasm probably cut by the actions of preglacial streams. Another result of such stream action was the creation of outliers, large sections of escarpment that have become separated from the main scarp and stand off on their own. Rattlesnake Point, which can be reached on this walk, is located on the Milton Outlier.

Start off your walk with a visit to the Indian village and then circle Crawford Lake. There are interpretive displays around this meromictic lake (a deep, narrow lake that lacks oxygen in its bottom layers), explaining both its natural and settlement history. After completing the lake loop, pick up the Woodland Trail (red markers), heading east. At the first trail junction, continue straight ahead on the Pine Ridge Trail (green markers). You will shortly get a fine view of Mount Nemo, after which the trail continues through a meadow, past a picturesque barn and into a woods.

At the next trail junction, turn right onto the main Bruce Trail (white blazes) and walk to the Niagara Escarpment Lookout. At this spot, you can often watch turkey vultures soaring by at eye level.

From the lookout, walk west along the edge of the escarpment to the next trail junction. At the junction, turn right and descend into Nassagaweya Canyon. Follow the white blazes through the canyon for about a kilometre. At the south end of the trail in the canyon, it turns left, crosses Limestone Creek and then passes by a buffalo compound. Five buffalo were originally brought here in 1965 from Wood Buffalo National Park in Alberta and they have thrived since, with so many offspring that the herd has had to be split in two.

130

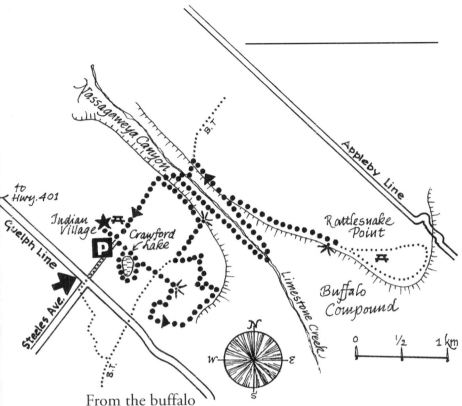

From the buffalo
compound, continue to follow the white blazes as the trail
gently climbs out of the canyon. At the next junction, turn
right onto the blue-blazed Bruce Trail side trail that heads
across the Milton Outlier to Rattlesnake Point.

As you walk toward the point, you will have fine views
of the canyon on your right. At the Nassagaweya Lookout
(marked by a metal fence), the blue side trail ends. You can
now turn back and return to Crawford Lake or continue
along a park trail to the picnic area in the Rattlesnake Point
Conservation Area. Follow the yellow markers to reach the
picnic ground and, after lunch, backtrack to the lookout point.

From the lookout point, return to Crawford Lake on
the blue side trail. At the point where the blue-blazed side
trail and the white-blazed main trail meet, follow the white
trail until you once again see blue blazes. At that point,
switch back to the blue. From here, turn left and follow the
blue blazes down the escarpment. You will now be on the

Jack Leech-Porter Side Trail, which cuts straight across the canyon through a cedar swamp on a series of boardwalks. (In spring, make sure to bring some insect repellent!) Once you reach the opposite side of the canyon, the blue blazes will end. Turn right and follow the white blazes up the escarpment. Stay right until you see the blue blazes marking the Steeles Avenue Side Trail. You should see some fine examples of mature white pines along this section. Follow this trail through the woods back to the Conservation Centre at Crawford Lake.

Credit Valley Footpath

Old Hydro Station
Credit Valley Footpath.

LENGTH: 16.5 kilometres
TIME: 5 hours
TERRAIN: Mostly level, but with some steep ascents. Footing can be wet and slippery.
DIRECTIONS: From Highway 401, take exit 333 and follow Regional Road 19 (Winston Churchill Boulevard) north to Highway 7. Turn east on Highway 7 and look for an old gas station (now a florist shop) on the north side of the highway. Leave one vehicle here. Return west on Highway 7 to the village of Norval. At the stoplight, turn north on Regional Road 19 and drive until you reach Old School Road. Turn left and, when you reach the 10th Line, turn right. Follow 10th Line north to where the Bruce Trail (white blazes) crosses it. Look for a private estate with buildings featuring white walls and red roofs near the junction. Leave your vehicle well off to the side on 10th Line.

Anyone looking to spend a full day walking in the country should consider this walk. You will have to arrange a car shuttle if you're intent on going the entire distance—you would have to run to have time to backtrack. However, if you can't arrange to have a vehicle at either end or you just want a somewhat shorter outing, consider parking at the lot opposite the Old Paper Mill bridge, crossing the dam and walking south to the old hydro station before returning on the same route to your car.

Whatever route you choose to take, please remember that this footpath runs over private land. Stay on the trail, keep your dog on a leash and leave nothing behind. As well, make sure to bring a lunch and drinking water.

The trail runs mostly along the rim of the Credit Valley, but occasionally dips down into it. Some spots in the bottom lands can be constantly wet, even in dry weather, while in wet weather, the red clay that other sections run on can become extremely slippery. Wear boots and watch your footing.

At the south end of the footpath, park your car near the old gas station that is currently a florist shop just east of the town of Norval on the north side of Highway 7. As you face this building, the footpath is blazed (blue blazes) along the old road allowance running directly to the right of the building.

To start the walk from the north end, walk south from the junction of the main Bruce Trail (white blazes) and the 10th Line toward Old School Road, where the trail turns right, crosses a stile and enters the Sheridan Nurseries property, becoming in the process a true footpath. The trail heads uphill through a cedar bush, up a steep slope to a promontory. According to the *Bruce Trail Guidebook*, "the grassy mounds here are the site of an old Indian burial ground which should not be disturbed." From here the trail continues along the edge of the slope and passes a cemetery before reaching 20 Side Road.

The trail crosses the side road and enters a hardwood bush of maple, birch and poplar. After crossing a nursery access road, the trail cuts through a field, re-enters the woods and then descends into the river valley. In the valley, trees such as willow, ash and cedar are more common and bracken and ostrich fern grow thickly along the river. Here the trail crosses property owned by the Georgetown Golf Club, including a small creek, before reaching the Credit River. You'll have to pay close attention through this stretch, as the dense growth of ferns and thistles can make the path difficult to find in July and August.

The trail continues to follow the river bank and passes through a marshy area that can become quite wet, depending on the flow of the river. The trail runs out of the marsh

135

up a steep bank and then along a golf club road. It then quickly leaves the road, turning left into a ravine, crossing a bridge and climbing up into drier mixed woodlands. From the woods, the trail crosses a stile into a field and then skirts the old head pond of the paper mill. The trail crosses a fence again and then runs under the new bridge to Old Paper Mill bridge (now for pedestrians only). Across the river is the access point for the shorter walk.

From the old bridge, the trail climbs up to the top edge of the valley again and follows the Credit River Gorge. After passing under a CNR viaduct, the trail drops down to the remains of an old hydro station, a lovely piece of architecture and a good place for lunch. After this, the trail once again leaves the valley and comes to a junction with a side trail (yellow blazes) leading to the 10th Line road allowance. Instead of following this side trail, follow the blue blazes onto the property of Upper Canada College and into an old meadow studded with apple trees and hawthorns. This is a good place to look for yellow warblers (nesting), northern orioles (eating) or woodcock (mating flights). Watch out for poison ivy, however.

The trail then descends to the river and passes by a metal footbridge, which links the college to its outdoor education school. When it reaches a fence line, the trail turns left and follows the fence to Peel Regional Road 19. The trail then follows the regional road south, turns east on Old Pine Crest Road and then continues downhill on a road allowance to the access point east of Norval described above.

Forks of the Credit
Provincial Park

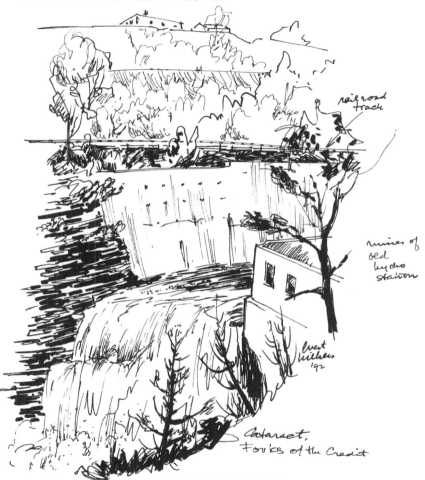

railroad track

ruines of old hydro station

Great Withers 192

Cataract, Forks of the Credit

LENGTH: 7 kilometres
TIME: 3 hours
TERRAIN: Rolling terrain, with two steep ascents
DIRECTIONS: Turn west on Caledon 2nd Line West from Highway 24 (just north of the town of Caledon). Look for the sign indicating Forks of the Credit Provincial Park parking. Parking is free.

The Forks of the Credit area has a well-deserved reputation for being one of the most beautiful areas for walking within easy access of Toronto. In fact, if the area has a drawback, it may be that, especially in the fall when the colours here are brilliant, it can be too popular. That said, many of those who come to the area are sightseers who barely get more than 20 metres from their cars; most days the trails of this park offer quiet and seclusion.

Our route saves the best for last. Start off on Access Trail A, which runs to the left of Kettle Lake. (A kettle lake is a lake created by glaciation that has no in- or outflow. Instead, a pocket carved in rock by glaciers is filled with meltwater and, later, rainwater to form a small self-contained lake.) Cross the Meadow Trail by walking under the telephone lines and keep on the A trail until you reach the Bruce Trail, which is identified by a diamond on a post. Turn left (east) and follow the white blazes into the woods.

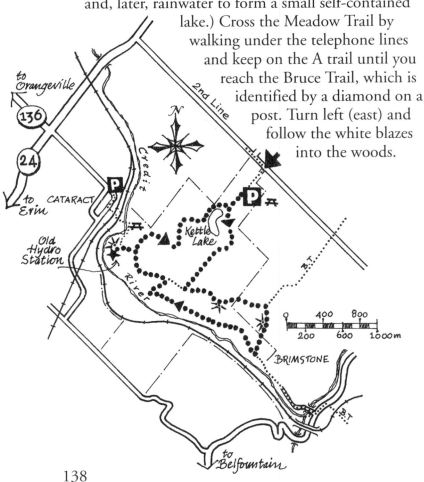

Stop to admire the fine view of the Credit Valley through the trees on your right.

The Bruce Trail will eventually lead you out of the woods onto a dirt road where you will notice a double white blaze. At this point, turn right onto the Bruce Trail side trail marked with blue blazes. Now you will have an unobstructed view of the valley on your left. The side trail descends through a woods into the valley and emerges at Dominion Road. Turn right on the road and once again follow the white blazes of the main Bruce Trail. Follow the road until you come to a sign that says that the trail ahead has been closed due to dangerous conditions. Turn right and follow the Bruce Trail (white blazes and park signs) up the hill. This is a steep ascent. At the top of the hill is a trail junction (and an orange garbage can); turn left and head toward the waterfalls and the viewing platform, while taking the time to enjoy the views off to your left—and to catch your breath.

At the next junction, go left and take the stairs down to the viewing platform and a newly installed interpretive display. From here, you can see the cataract and the old hydro station that provided power to customers of the Cataract Electric Company in a radius of 8 kilometres, starting in 1899. Before that, the building used by Cataract was a flour mill, served by the railway that still uses the picturesque trestle bridge over the Credit, and, prior to that, a sawmill. Many visitors come straight to the falls from the parking lot just above, so this can be a busy spot.

After admiring the falls, head back up the 163 steps to the trail junction up top and then continue straight along the park trail (toward the silo). You will see the meadow on your right. When you reach the Meadow Trail (look for the telephone line), turn right and walk along it until you reach Access Trail B. Turn left on the B trail and follow it along the opposite shore of Kettle Lake back to your car. There are picnic tables and outhouses along the river near the falls as well as near the parking lot at Kettle Lake.

Glen Haffy

The Dingle School

LENGTH: 7 kilometres
TIME: 3 ½ hours
TERRAIN: Rolling hills, with three stiles to cross
DIRECTIONS: The conservation area is located 10 kilometres north of Caledon East on Airport Road. Park in the Lookout Point parking lot. Not transit accessible. There is a small day-use fee.

Glen Haffy is located in the northwest corner of the Toronto bioregion, where the Oak Ridges Moraine meets the Niagara Escarpment. This is an important water recharge area for the Humber River, with creeks feeding run-off from both the escarpment and the moraine into the river.

The Glen Haffy area presents hikers with lots of options: walk just the conservation area nature trail (which

140

takes about one hour); combine the trail with the Dingle Loop off the Bruce Trail; or even continue from the junction of the Dingle and Bruce trails on the Albion Hills Side Trail through Palgrave Forest to Albion Hills Conservation Area (10.5 km one way). All the trails are well-marked dirt paths. The Glen Haffy Conservation Area itself has picnic areas, outhouses, barbecues and stocked fishing ponds.

For a pleasant half-day walk in a quiet rural setting, start off on the nature trail from the Lookout Point parking lot. Descend the steps to the trail junction and then go right on the red trail (red arrows), which shares its right-of-way with the Bruce Trail (white blazes). When this joint trail exits the woods, don't turn right on the red trail, but continue straight on the Bruce Trail, which skirts the woods until it reaches 35 Side Road. Climb the stile (fence ladder) and cross the road. Enter the woods on the other side while following the white blazes up a laneway. Soon you will arrive at a trail junction. The Albion Hills Side Trail breaks off to your left and the Dingle Loop Trail is on your right. Climb the stile on your right and follow the blue blazes marking the Dingle Trail. This trail meanders through a pleasant forest of mature yellow birch, hemlock and maple and crosses a small brook that is one of the headwaters of the Humber River.

The trail through the dingle (a deep, narrow valley) eventually loops back to the laneway from which you originally joined it. Climb over the stile and turn left onto the laneway, which is unmarked. Do not follow the blue blazes to the right or you will take yourself well out of your way. As you walk down the laneway, you will come across the picturesque Dingle School on your right. (The school is now a private residence.) The laneway will also take you past the stile over which you originally climbed to reach the Dingle Trail, and then carries on to 35 Side Road. Cross the road and reenter the conservation area by following the white blazes back to the junction where you broke away from the red trail. Rejoin the red trail, going left in the direction of the arrow. This trail will lead you back to Lookout Point. Along the way, there are some nice picnic spots with good views of the countryside. At Lookout Point there are benches for enjoying the vista before you finally return to your car.

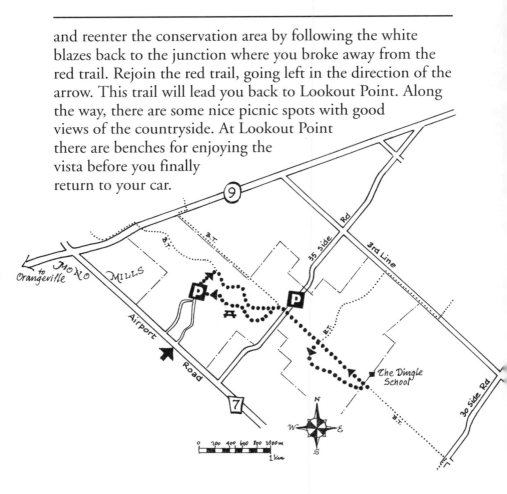

142

Hilton Falls
Conservation Area

Hilton Falls –
Pothole

Ehut Hillers

LENGTH: 9.5 kilometres
TIME: 4 hours
TERRAIN: Mostly flat, but the trail itself varies from a wide gravel path to a rocky trail. Be sure to wear sturdy footwear.
DIRECTIONS: From Highway 401, take Highway 25 north to Regional Road 9. Go west on Regional Road 9 for 6 kilometres to the conservation area entrance. There is a small day-use fee.

The Hilton Falls Conservation Area in the Halton County
Forest is a good example of the link between habitat and
species. Because the conservation area has such varied habitat, from soft-maple swamp forests to upland hardwood bush
to beaver meadow, it also supports a great variety of wildlife.
One of its most interesting residents is the West Virginia
white butterfly, a rare species that is particularly demanding
in its habitat needs. These include large, uninterrupted tracts
of hardwood forest and, in its larval stage, toothwort, a plant
that is uncommon in Ontario.

For walkers, the conservation area offers an excellent
system of seven stacked trail loops, so you can
walk as little or as much as you want. Along
the way, there's bound to be lots to see.
Close to one hundred species of birds
have been seen in the area, including
twenty-two types of warblers
(including Nashville and
blackburnian).

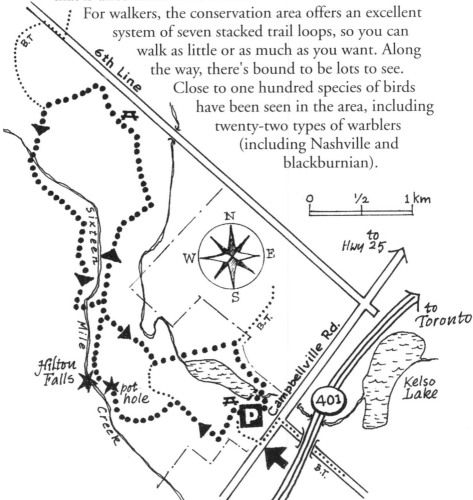

Knock on an old, cavity-filled tree along the trail and a northern flying squirrel might stick its head out—or even take a flying leap. The wetland areas support four different types of salamanders, making this one of the few areas in North America where all four are found together. Another unusual wetlands visitor to watch for is the American water shrew. As well, the Hilton Falls area supports a good number of white-tailed deer, a beaver colony and plenty of porcupines.

From the parking lot, walk behind the visitor centre to the service road and enter the woods at the trail sign. Follow the Hilton Falls Trail (yellow markers) and watch for the blue blazes indicating a Bruce Trail side trail. Turn left onto the side trail and follow the blue blazes toward the falls. Before you reach the falls, however, the trail passes a rock pothole where a sign has been posted explaining this geological phenomenon. Continue on to the falls after you've studied the pothole. There is another interpretive display, as well as picnic tables and a fire ring, at the falls.

The falls are created by a branch of Sixteen Mile Creek pouring over the edge of the Niagara Escarpment. Early settlers quickly recognized their potential. Between 1835 and 1867, three separate sawmills were built near the falls. None of the mills lasted long, however. All three were either quickly abandoned or burned down. Hilton Falls is now part of the United Nation's Niagara Escarpment Biosphere Reserve.

When you leave the falls, continue north alongside the creek on the Hilton Falls Side Trail. Plants to watch for in the woods include yellow lady's-slipper and walking fern. The trail emerges from the woods at a 6-foot-wide gravel path. Turn left and follow the Beaver Dam Trail (orange markers). At the next trail junction, go right and walk along the broad track following the orange markers; the blue-blazed side trail joins this trail where you cross the stream so it is marked for some distance with both orange arrows and blue blazes.

The Beaver Dam Trail passes through an early successional forest of maple, poplar and birch. It's dry underfoot through here, the walking is pleasant, and there are lots of reptiles and amphibians to be seen if you move quietly, so bring your field guide. At about the halfway point of the loop there is a picnic table and a fire ring. A short distance after this, the Hilton Falls Side Trail (blue blazes) goes off to the right to join the main Bruce Trail, approximately 4 kilometres to the north. Our walk, however, continues on the Beaver Dam Trail (orange arrows) and completes the circle around the beaver meadow.

At this point the track begins to narrow and becomes a dirt trail and crosses Sixteen Mile Creek over a culvert. This crossing can be a problem in the spring or after a heavy rain; it can be knee-deep in water. Check with park staff before heading out to see if the crossing is passable or be prepared to wade. The nice thing is that the trail ahead is worth the effort; it continues through a pleasant woods and offers both solitude and views of wildlife.

The trail recrosses the creek on a good bridge—you can see the beaver dam from here—and returns to the trail junction. Turn right or you will end up going around the loop again. Follow the orange markers until you see the red markers for the Red Oak Trail and then turn left. Stay left and cross the creek just above where it empties into the reservoir and then turn right onto the Bruce Trail (white blazes) for a fine view of both the reservoir and the creek. If you happen to be visiting after a heavy rain, you will get to see how the swollen creek creates impressive white-water chutes as it tumbles into the reservoir.

Continue a short way on the Bruce Trail until it rejoins the Red Oak Trail and bends to the right around the reservoir. At this point, the Bruce Trail turns left and leads to the Dufferin Quarry Bridge. Stay on the red-marker trail instead, going right across the dam (built in the early 1970s for flood control) and then left behind the visitors' centre to return to the parking lot.

Lower Oakville Creek (Sixteen Mile Creek)

Event Walkers

Oakville Creek
Bridge over Hwy 5

LENGTH: 11 kilometres
TIME: 4 hours
TERRAIN: Mostly level, but with some steep ascents and descents. The trail is informal and unmarked and occasionally crosses areas of red clay that can be very slippery when wet.
DIRECTIONS: If you're coming by car, you will probably want to arrange a shuttle, as there is no way (except by backtracking from a midpoint) to shorten the walk and it makes for a long round trip. To reach the starting point, watch for the sign for the Lions Park on Highway 5 (Dundas Street) just to the east of Oakville Creek. Follow the access road under the highway to the free parking area. The park closes at eight p.m. It has washrooms, picnic tables and a playground. To reach the finishing point, take Highway 5 east to Trafalgar Road; Trafalgar south to Upper Middle Road; Upper Middle west until it curves and becomes

McCraney Road. Park in the clearing under the hydro lines.
There is no access by transit.

This walk may be at its best in the spring when a number of
interesting forest plants and flowers are in bloom. But if you
choose to come through here later in the year, you certainly
won't be alone; many fishermen come angling for coho salmon
in the creek each fall. The creek valley itself was central to the
white-oak woodlands that once covered this area and from
which the town of Oakville took its name. There aren't a lot
of big trees left, but there is an interesting mixture of flora
and fauna to be seen in the valley and on the tablelands above.

 Starting from the Lions Park parking lot, head south
along the informal trail through the flood plain. The remnant
fruit trees of some old orchards are scattered through this
section—another possible reason to come through in fall. The
trail crosses over a small brook before climbing up from the
flood plain and onto a narrow ridge. The higher ground is
dominated by white pine, oaks and sugar maples with a thick
understorey of shrubs, including snowberry, serviceberry and
blueberry.

 The path then descends the front slope of the ridge
to the river valley floor. Near the river it breaks left sharply

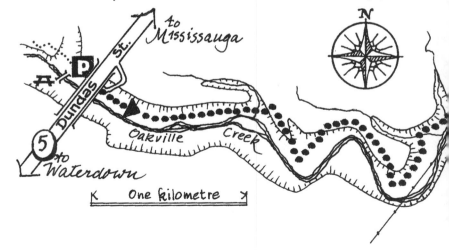

148

and heads back toward higher ground again, climbing up onto another of the pointed outcrops created by the steep-sided tributary ravines that regularly intersect the main valley. Before you leave the valley, however, take time to study some of the plants growing in this bottom-land forest of black maple and white ash. Among those to look for are twin-leaf, Virginia bluebells, Dutchman's-breeches and hepatica. Mixed in with the ashes and oaks, you will also see some substantial sugar maples and the occasional basswood and butternut tree, as well. On the drier tableland of the ridge separating the tributary valley and the main Oakville Creek channel, a forest of red and white oak, sugar maple, white pine and the occasional black cherry predominates. Follow along the southern edge of the ridge until you enter a clearing at the top of a bluff. This is an excellent lookout point for the entire valley, and you may even see red-tailed hawks soaring past.

From the clearing, follow an old trail down and across the slope. For those walking the trail in the spring, this section should be carpeted in trout lilies. Keep following the trail along the bottom of the slope once you reach the flood plain. Shortly, you will have to cross another small brook flowing out of another side valley. It's a very mixed forest through this section, and in the springtime it features a beautiful carpet of forest flowers, including trilliums and trout lilies, to add to your enjoyment.

The trail crosses the brook, then follows it for a piece toward Oakville Creek, coming out into a more open flood-plain community made up of such pioneer species as willow and dogwood. For the first time in a while, you will actually be walking close to the banks of the creek and will have a chance to observe the power of its flow or, in the fall, the amazing salmon migration.

Just before crossing one more tributary brook, you enter an interesting forest with some uncommon southern species, including bitternut hickory and blue beech. This forest thrives thanks to the rich soils and shelter of the valley.

149

Along here is also another good stretch on which to see spring flowers.

After crossing the brook, the path cuts close to a bend in the river marked by a wide limestone shelf notable for some interesting fossils. From here, the path cuts up the bluff on an angle. From the top, you will get a view of the Glen Abbey Golf Course before the path takes you away from the bluff edge, past a pumping station and along an access road to the end of Upper Middle Road.

Mount Nemo
Conservation Area

Mount Nemo

Evert hickens, 1992

LENGTH: 2.5 kilometres
TIME: 1 hour
TERRAIN: Flat, with one steep ascent. The trail along the top of the escarpment is rocky; wear sturdy footwear.
DIRECTIONS: From the QEW take Guelph Line (County Road 1) north to Colling Road. Park in the gravel lot on the northwest corner of the intersection or on the shoulder of Guelph Line.

Standing on the edge of the Niagara Escarpment at Mount Nemo, it's interesting to think about the forces that created this rocky ridge which, after lying buried to the south, rises into prominence in the landscape again here. The escarpment is actually what remains of the outer rim of a warm inland sea, centered in the state of Michigan, that existed some 400 million years ago. Layers of sand and sediment deposited by the sea's waters created some of the escarpment's lower layers of shale and sandstone. Lime-rich organic matter from the sea was also left behind to become today's layers of fossil-filled limestone. Finally, limestone and magnesium mixed to create the escarpment's hard cap, a rock structure known as dolomite.

Since its formation, the escarpment has been shaped by glaciers, water run-off and erosion. Throughout the Mount Nemo area, for example, the escarpment is crosscut with fissures created by the eroding action of small streams. In places, these fissures even begin to take on a cavelike structure. Slowly but surely, the escarpment continues to change. But for a moment, just think about what it would be like to be standing on top of Mount Nemo looking out over a vast saltwater sea.

This is a short walk, but those who want to extend it can simply continue in either direction on the main Bruce Trail. The views from the escarpment edge are spectacular at any time of year, and keep an eye out for turkey vultures spiralling in the updrafts created by the escarpment face.

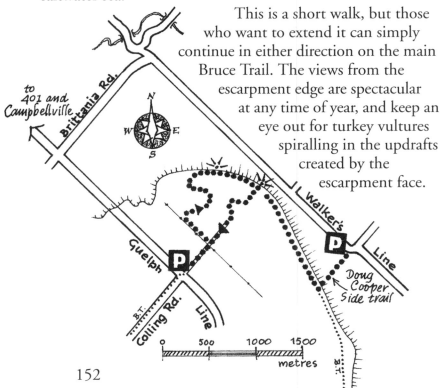

152

From the intersection of Guelph Line and Colling Road, walk east on the road allowance. When you arrive at a hydro pole marked with two white blazes indicating a change of direction of the main Bruce Trail, turn left and follow the footpath along a hydro line. The path will lead you into a shady maple-beech woods, a good place to admire woodland flowers in the springtime. The trail circles through the woods. Keep right at the two trail junctions you come to (both are marked with double white blazes) before proceeding up the escarpment edge. From here, there are fine views of the Crawford Lake Conservation Area and Rattlesnake Point, a prominent escarpment feature.

The trail continues along the escarpment edge to a man-made lookout point constructed of stone. There are good views off to the left along this entire section of trail. At the lookout, you will have to decide whether you want to continue for a ways on the Bruce Trail or whether you are ready to return to the starting point.

To return, turn west onto the road allowance and walk back to Guelph Line. You shouldn't have any problem recognizing the road allowance, but it is marked with blue blazes (Bruce Trail side trail) in any case.

An alternative to the above route is to start from the east side of Mount Nemo on Walker's Line. If you choose this option, park on the shoulder of the road near the park gate. Look for the yellow blazes indicating the Doug Cooper Side Trail. This is an 800-metre trail that makes a steep ascent through a rock fissure up to the main Bruce Trail (white blazes). When you reach the Bruce Trail, turn right and follow the white blazes to a road allowance. Turn left onto the road allowance and then right at the marked hydro pole to pass through the woods described above. From here, follow the trail along to the lookout point and then continue south on the main trail until you return to the junction with the Doug Cooper Trail, from which you can descend to your car.

Palgrave Forest

Palgrave - the end of the hike

LENGTH: 8.5 kilometres
TIME: 2 ¹/₂ hours
TERRAIN: Gently rolling hills, with wide mown-grass trails
DIRECTIONS: Palgrave Forest is just north of the town of
Palgrave on Highway 50. However, in the summer months,
the entrance off Highway 50 is used by logging trucks, so
continue to the north edge of the forest at 30 Side Road.
Turn left and take the side road west to 6th Line. Turn left
again (south) on 6th Line and look for an unmarked gravel
drive on your left (no mailbox or signage). Enter here and
park in the pull-off just outside the gate or, if the gate is
open, continue to the large parking lot.

The Palgrave Forest is a planted pine forest managed by the
Metropolitan Toronto and Region Conservation Authority
(MTRCA) and part of that management includes an active
program of cutting and replanting. Thanks to its location on
the Oak Ridges Moraine, we can be fairly certain that this
particular forest is growing on sandy, gravelly soils, conditions that are quite agreeable to red and white pine. In fact,
the practice of planting large tracts of pine on the moraine

dates back to the late 1930s and early 1940s when it became apparent that overcutting and farming had left the easily disturbed, silty soils of the moraine badly eroded. As Palgrave is relatively small and a popular cross-country ski area in winter, the cutting here doesn't tend to run to enormous clear-cuts. Still, whole areas, rather than selective trees, are cleared out to give shade-intolerant pine seedlings favourable growing conditions. White-tailed deer also seem to approve of the browse these clearings provide.

You can pick up the trail system at the southeast corner of the parking lot. Follow the red ski trail to the right, in the direction of the arrow. The trail will take you up to the top of a hill that affords a good view of the surrounding countryside and then continues into a reforested area. Approach this area quietly and watch for deer. The trail emerges from the woods again at a fence line, which it then follows. At the second junction with the blue trail, turn left and follow the blue trail back into the woods. Follow the blue trail to the winter-use parking lot and rejoin the red trail there. The red trail emerges from the woods after a kilometre or so to run alongside the Humber River. The Humber is the only river that actually runs across the Oak Ridges Moraine; otherwise the moraine serves as a watershed divide for streams running south to Lake Ontario and streams running north to Georgian Bay and Lake Simcoe.

Shortly after the red trail joins the Humber, the Humber passes through a wet meadow that's a great place to practice your herpetology skills—in other words, to look for frogs and snakes. This is also an interesting spot to explore the kinds of plants that grow in such boggy conditions and a good place to stop and bird-watch if the bugs aren't too bad.

From here, the red trail wanders around the perimeter of the property through more stands of pine reforestation. Along the west side of the property, notice how the forest edges are filling in with flowering shrubs such as multiflora rosa, elderberry and honeysuckle. These should be particularly pretty in June. On the other hand, with its overlooks and rich pine smells, this could also be a very pleasant walk to do in the fall. As well, for those who want a longer walk, the Bruce Trail (look for the white blazes on the 6th Line) will take you west to the Glen Haffy Conservation Area (approximately 6 kilometres) or south to the Albion Hills Conservation Area (2 kilometres), where more trails can be explored.

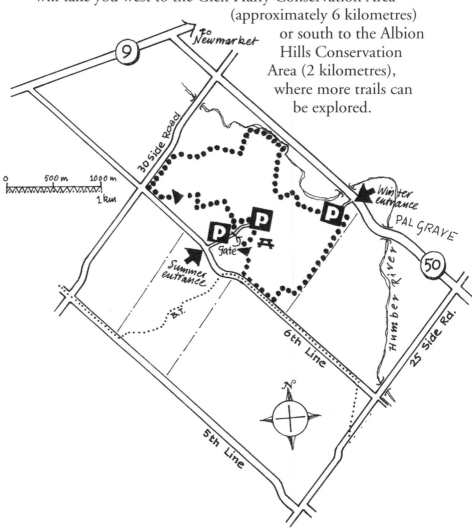

Royal Botanical Gardens – Cootes Paradise North Shore Trails

LENGTH: 6 kilometres
TIME: 3 ¹/₂ - 4 hours
TERRAIN: Gently rolling hills, with one or two steep ascents (stairs provided). Trails are generally wide and well groomed.
DIRECTIONS: From Highway 403, take Highway 6 north to York Road, then York Road west to the parking lot marked North Shore Trails. By transit, take Hamilton city bus Rock Gardens 9 to the Royal Botanical Gardens (RBG) entrance.

The North Shore Trails of Cootes Paradise crisscross an area that in the late 1700s was a wildlife paradise known to only a few settlers and to Captain Thomas Cootes. While the sheer numbers of birds and animals that Cootes saw certainly don't exist here today, this area is still abundant and diverse. This walk alone passes through meadow, forest, marsh, cultivated gardens, wildflower gardens and a native tree display. Before even beginning the walk, we saw a juvenile northern mockingbird being fed by an adult. This a great place for birds, botany and butterflies.

Leave the parking lot by following the Bruce Trail side trail (blue blazes) east. As you walk along, you will also see signs for the RBG's Pinetum Trail, which shares the same track. Follow the two trails east (left) through a meadow until you reach the Macdonell Trail. At this well-signed junction, turn right. In the meadow on your right are man-made nesting boxes for bluebirds or tree swallows and a kestrel box. To your left is the edge of a hardwood bush. The trail passes under some hydro wires and then enters the woods. Eventually you will come to a sign for the Macdonell Trail, pointing right toward a narrow track—don't follow it. Instead, remain on the main trail (a mown-grass strip) and you will soon reach a signpost where the Macdonell and Captain Cootes trails meet. Continue straight ahead on the Captain Cootes Trail until, after a short distance, you come to the Marsh Walk Trail. Turn right onto the Marsh Trail and you will gradually descend to the water's edge.

When you reach a signpost pointing in both directions for the Marsh Trail, go right and follow the boardwalk through a cattail marsh. At the viewing platform, look out over the whole of Cootes Paradise. Consider that, in the 1930s, more than 65 percent of Cootes was cattail marsh, not the brown, murky water seen today. Current marsh conditions are the result of the introduction of carp, which stir up sediment and uproot plants, the dumping of sewage and other toxins into the marsh, and fluctuating lake levels.

However, the RBG has embarked on an ambitious project to restore the cattail marsh—and the species that depend on it—with hand plantings, temporary fencing and log booms, and a permanent carp barrier between Cootes and Hamilton Harbour.

From the viewing platform, return to the signpost and turn right onto the asphalt treadway before rejoining the Captain Cootes Trail, where you turn right. The pleasant woodland that this stretch of trail leads through is full of birds. Look and listen for cardinals, white-breasted nuthatches, house wrens and catbirds, among others. Next you will reach a signpost with a bench in front of it. Follow the arrow pointing toward Bull's Point, where there is a lookout tower. Return from the tower back to the signpost and once again turn right on the Captain Cootes Trail.

The trail will shortly cross Lyn Valley Brook. On your right, you should now see some old pilings that stake out the former route of the Desjardins Canal. Built in the 1800s to link Dundas to the harbour, it was abandoned by the 1880s. Today, cormorants sometimes use the pilings as roosts.

The trail continues across Hickory Brook. Stay to the right, passing through a stand of sycamore trees, another reminder that Cootes is part of the endangered Carolinian life zone of southwestern Ontario. In fact, Cootes is close to the northern limit of where such sun-loving southern species as sycamore, black walnut and sassafras trees currently grow in Canada.

This area has become a popular year-round feeding ground for chickadees, so come prepared to offer some sunflower seeds. Even nuthatches and downy woodpeckers will perch on your hand to be fed here.

Continue over the boardwalk and then turn left up the stairs to the world-famous Lilac Dell, which blooms in late May, early June. There are benches in the dell, so this can be a good spot to eat lunch. Afterwards, climb south and east toward the water out of the dell and past the George E. Campbell collection of redbud trees, which flower in June. Follow the sign for the Captain Cootes Trail and then go left and walk along the shore where there is an interpretive display explaining the history of the Desjardins Canal.

The Captain Cootes Trail continues past a plant nursery and then turns left at a boathouse, where you can rent a canoe if you're so inclined. Soon after the boathouse, leave the Captain Cootes Trail and go right along a gravel road, walking carefully past the bee yard on your right.

Continue up the road to the Highland Creek Ravine Wild Plant Garden. Turn left to enter the garden and then, after you've had a chance to enjoy its offerings, cross Highland Creek via the wooden bridge and return to the Captain Cootes Trail. After rejoining the trail, turn right and walk up the hill through the rhododendron collection, which flowers from May to June to the nature centre.

Behind the centre is the George W. North Memorial Wildlife Garden, which demonstrates how you can create a backyard that attracts wildlife by choosing plants that are both attractive and functional. North was an avid bird-watcher and honourary member of the Hamilton Naturalists Club, which dedicated these gardens to his memory. The garden is visited by many birds, butterflies (particularly red admirals) and chipmunks.

As you leave the garden, turn left, cross the traffic circle and head across the lawn toward the large oak with a big rock in front of it. This is the starting point of a Bruce Trail side trail (blue blazes). You will see Rasberry House, the Bruce Trail Association's headquarters, on your right and also the remains of a stone silo covered in climbing roses. Follow the blue side trail through the Pinetum (a labelled conifer collection) along the gravel road back to your car.

See map on pages 162-63.

Royal Botanical Gardens – Hendrie Valley

Grindstone Creek
Y trail, South of Lambs Hollow

LENGTH: 6 kilometres
TIME: 2 hours
TERRAIN: Mostly level, with optional steep ascents to Laking Garden and RBG Rose Garden
DIRECTIONS: From Highway 403, take Plains Road to Botanical Drive, then right onto Spring Gardens Road. Free parking in the lot off Spring Gardens Road. By transit, take the Hamilton city bus, Rock Gardens 9.

As a nature reserve, the Hendrie Valley section of the Royal Botanical Gardens has a lot to offer. Thanks to the twists and turns of ancient glaciers, the area has been left with a wide diversity of plant and animal habitat, ranging from wetlands and acidic, sandy soils to richly forested slopes. The area also has a long human history, beginning with native trails that

161

crisscrossed the valley, possibly to join Iroquois settlements on the Niagara Escarpment to Burlington Bay.

Later, United Empire Loyalists settled in the area, and the valley became a major intersection for people moving between Hamilton and Toronto. Snake Road, which followed the route of the present-day Tollhouse Trail, was the route taken by wagons and stagecoaches over the escarpment— after, of course, they had paid their toll. In the 1870s, William Hendrie, a Scottish immigrant who grew wealthy through his involvement with the expansion of the railways, began to accumulate land and eventually acquired close to half the valley.

From the parking lot off Spring Gardens Road, start off on the Tollhouse Trail. Walking along the trail, you will come to an observation deck and bench offering a fine view of Grindstone Creek. Water levels in the creek can be quite variable due to large run-offs from the surrounding urban areas after rainstorms. Next, you will come to a staircase on your left leading up to the Laking Gardens, for which there is a charge in season. The gardens are at their best in May and June when the peonies and irises are in blossom.

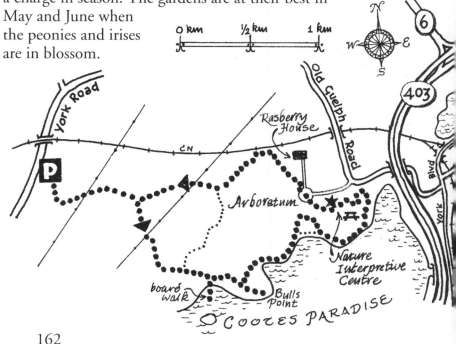

Follow the Tollhouse Trail under Highway 2 and continue along on a boardwalk. Along here, keep an eye out for interesting birds. Unfortunately, just after this point, the boardwalk ends at a brook and a definitely unscenic small tire dump. Cross the brook, however, and you can continue along the trail on the other side. Keep to the right.

A little further along, you will see a sign for the Yellowjacket Trail, which runs along the south slope of the valley, a slope dominated by warmth-loving oak and hickory trees. Follow the Yellowjacket Trail and you will next arrive at an observation platform with a view over a marsh. After taking some time to see what's happening in the reeds, continue to the next signpost.

At this junction, you can cut the walk short by turning right or continue straight. For those continuing straight on, just ahead is a patch of Turk's cap lilies, which flower in July. After that, watch for the next signpost, where you stay with the right-hand trail. (The left branch goes to a private residence.)

As you walk along, you will come to a bridge arching over Grindstone Creek. Cross the bridge and turn left to walk through Lamb's Hollow. (Ragweed is plentiful here in August.) In this end of the valley, sun-loving plants thrive in rich soils. Walk through the meadow and cross Unsworth Avenue, following the bicycle path on the other side along the creek until you see Hidden Valley Park on your left. Cross over to the park

163

and enjoy a picnic. Along the creek here, in July, you can see pink touch-me-nots, a giant magenta-flowered relative of our native yellow and orange touch-me-nots.

After you've enjoyed a break, return as you came, back over Unsworth Avenue and through Lamb's Hollow, right back to the arched bridge over Grindstone Creek. Cross the bridge and rejoin Yellowjacket Trail, turning left as you leave the bridge. Follow the trail until you reach another bridge where there is a trail junction. Here you can cross the bridge and either go right to follow the Brackenbrae Trail back to the Tollhouse Trail or go left on the Brackenbrae Trail, across a boardwalk and into a forest of hemlock, maple and beech.

This bit of trail is cool and refreshing after the more exposed Yellowjacket Trail, and some of the trees in this section of the valley must date from before the arrival of the Loyalists. There are also some nice views of the South Pasture Swamp. As you go along, keep to the right to stay with the main trail, which will lead you to another trail junction, this one marked by a bench.

At this junction, your choice is to go left on the Bridle Path to Cherry Hill Gate and the Rose Garden (best in June and July, though there is a charge in season) or right to continue on the Brackenbrae Trail. If you continue on the Brackenbrae Trail, at the next signpost, turn left onto the Yellowjacket Trail and follow it as it crosses Grindstone Creek by bridge and boardwalk. At the next trail junction, turn left onto the Tollhouse Trail and return to the parking lot near Spring Gardens Road.

164

Sawmill Creek

to Springbank Centre

St. Peter's Anglican 1887

Dundas + Mississauga Rd, looking East

LENGTH: 9 kilometres
TIME: 2 hours
TERRAIN: Flat
DIRECTIONS: By transit: on weekdays and Saturdays, take the Mississauga Transit 1 bus from the Islington Subway Station, and on Sundays, the Mississauga Transit 101 bus. Get off when the bus turns north on Mississauga Road at the Collegeway stop. By car: take Dundas Street West (Highway 5) to Mississauga Road. Turn north on Mississauga Road and park on the east side of the road between the Springbank Centre and the church.

For walkers, this route puts its best features up front. The first half of the loop takes you through a forested valley with a nice selection of Carolinian tree species such as black walnut, blue beech and shagbark hickory. To the northwest of Burnhamthorpe Road, the route is somewhat lacking in natural features, but still makes for pleasant enough walking and a nice alternative to backtracking.

Starting from the Springbank Centre, cross Mississauga Road to the west side and walk north on the asphalt trail under Collegeway until you reach the Sawmill Valley Trail. (If you've arrived by transit, the trail is marked at the northwest corner of Mississauga Road and Collegeway.) On your right, just as you follow the trail into the woods, there is a well-established trumpet vine, which throws out spectacular flowers in August.

As you walk through the southern end of the valley, you will notice a number of fine examples of warmth-loving black walnut trees, which thrive in the rich valley soils. Mixed in with the dominant walnuts are blue beech trees (more commonly found on Pelee Island), butternut, black cherry and shagbark hickory. Breaking from the very southerly forest appearance of these hardwoods is a stand of white pine on a rise after a small bridge.

Throughout the valley, there is a rich understorey of forest plants, including such spring ephemerals as trilliums and toothwort (the host plant for the larvae of the rare West Virginia white butterfly). For wildlife, in addition to the food source of nuts provided by the hickory and walnut trees, there are also good berry crops to be found on shrubs such as red-osier dogwood, elderberry and chokecherry. Another interesting shrub found in the valley is witch hazel, often found growing near the creek.

Just before Burnhamthorpe Road, the trail leaves the woods and enters a meadow. Black-eyed Susans are one of the plants that stand out in this old field community of clover, wild carrot, milkweed and thistles.

Follow the trail under Burnhamthorpe Road. At the trail junction, turn left and cross over the ditch before turning left again (look for the Sawmill Valley Trail sign) and reentering the woods. While black walnut saplings are common on the southern slopes here, the make-up of the forest on the northwest side of the creek is a little different from that seen in the southern part of the valley. Here, the more commonly found community of sugar maple and red and white oaks predominates.

To make a loop, continue on the path under the Erin Mills Parkway and then turn right as it leads you behind a set of apartment buildings. At the next trail junction, stay left and then turn left again and climb the hill behind the townhouses. At the top, make a sharp left and walk under Burnhamthorpe Road toward Loyola Secondary School. On the opposite side of the road, turn left again and then right onto South Common Court. Walk to the end of the court and take the asphalt path just to the right of the church. Turn right immediately and walk alongside the school. Staying with the footpath, keep right at the next trail junction and enter the woods.

At the next trail junction, you will see an apartment building directly ahead. At this point, turn left and left again to walk between the rows of townhouses. You are now on the Glen Erin Trail. Follow the trail under Collegeway and across Council Ring Road to the Brookmede Centre. Here you will see a children's playground on your right.

Follow the trail to the left between an earthen berm and more townhouses, then cross 5th Line West and continue walking behind the Millway Shopping Centre.

From here, the trail continues under the Erin Mills Parkway. Shortly, you will come to a wooden bridge on your left leading across Sawmill Creek to Windy Hollow Park, a nice spot for a picnic. Return across the bridge from Windy Hollow and turn left to continue on the Glen Erin Trail until you reach Collegeway. At Collegeway, turn right and follow the road over the Sawmill Valley Trail and then turn right again, passing through the ruins of the Glen Erin Hall Gatehouse as you go. Cross Mississauga Road and you will have returned to the starting point.

Terra Cotta
Conservation Area

LENGTH: Approximately 6 kilometres
TIME: 4 hours
TERRAIN: Gently rolling hills. Trails range from well marked to unmarked. The Bruce Trail, which is used for part of this walk, runs mostly over red clay, which can be very slippery when wet.
DIRECTIONS: From Highway 10, take Regional Road 9 (intersection in the town of Victoria) west to Regional Road 19 (Winston Churchill Boulevard). Enter off of Regional Road 19 just northwest of the town of Terra Cotta. Park at the visitor services centre. There is a small day-use fee.

According to a history provided by the Credit Valley Conservation Authority, the town for which this conservation area is named used to be known as Salmonville. By the late 1800s, however, the Atlantic salmon that gave the town its name were gone from the Credit River and the town's name was changed to Terra Cotta in honour of the red clay deposits in the area, which are used to this day for pottery. And while the Credit River may no longer be rich in salmon, it is a clear and, at times, powerful stream fed by hundreds of springs and feeder streams that run off the Niagara Escarpment.

The Terra Cotta Conservation Area itself is a well-treed site that makes for pleasant walking at any time of year. If you only want a short—but interesting—stroll, you can walk the Alan F. Coventry Nature Trail, a 2-kilometre interpretive forest trail. But by combining a portion of the Coventry Nature Trail with stretches of the Bruce Trail and parts of various unmarked ski trails, you can get a better look at what this area has to offer.

Start the walk from the visitor services centre (open from one p.m. to four p.m. daily). Enter the Alan F. Coventry Nature Trail and stay to the left. As you walk along, observe the gradually maturing hardwood forest. Among the maple, oak and beech trees that are becoming dominant here, you can still find interesting southerly species such as shagbark hickory and bitternut hickory.

At interpretive post number 5, you'll notice that the blue blazes of the nature trail have been joined by the white blazes of the Bruce Trail. Follow the combined trail across a creek (a tributary of the Credit) until you come to a tree with a double white blaze (indicating a change in direction) that is close to a sign saying Nature Trail and pointing to the right. Here the two trails diverge. Follow the white blazes of the Bruce Trail to the left. You will now find yourself walking through a mature and deeply shaded maple, oak and beech forest. The trail leads out to a service road, where you can turn left and head down the road to use the group camping area for picnicing. The area combines a nice view with facilities such as picnic tables and outhouses.

When you've finished lunch, head back up the road to where you left the Bruce Trail. Reenter the woods on the opposite side of the road from the one you exited from and follow the Bruce Trail for approximately a kilometre before turning right onto an unmarked park trail known as the Main Trail. This is a mown-grass trail about 6 feet wide, and where it meets the Bruce Trail, there are double white blazes on either side of it. The Bruce Trail turns left here, leading down a hill and into a meadow where it leaves the park. There are two signs marking private property in the meadow, so if you see them, you know you've gone too far. If you do find yourself in the meadow, don't attempt to take a shortcut back to the Main Trail via the ski trail that leaves the meadow through the woods; it's overgrown with poison ivy!

From the junction, follow the Main Trail through the woods, ignoring the campground on your right and the many side trails

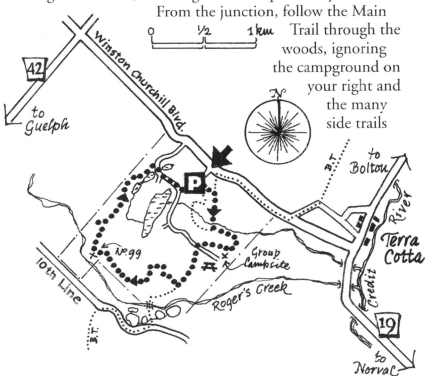

coming in on your left. The Main Trail exits the woods at campsite 99 in the campground. From here, follow the service road to the left and then rejoin the Main Trail as it re-enters the woods between campsites 83 and 84. On this section, the trail follows a wooded ridge above Roger's Creek. Watch carefully and take the first trail that goes off to the right (there are no markers). At the next trail junction, stay left. Continue on this trail as it goes down a hill and across a log culvert. You will finally emerge from the woods at Muskrat Pond, where you'll find a bench waiting for you to rest on. From here, turn left and walk out to the road and then turn right on the road and follow it back the visitor services centre.

Selected Bibliography

Beeby, Susan. "Rouge Rambles." *Seasons,* Vol. 30, No. 1. Federation of Ontario Naturalists, 1990.

Bruce Trail Association. *Guide to the Bruce Trail,* 18th Edition. Bruce Trail Association, 1992.

Department of Parks and Recreation. "Glen Stewart Ravine Nature Trail." (Pamphlet.) City of Toronto, 1992.

Higgins, Verna J., Susan Denzel, and Nancy Fazari. *Plant Communities of the Leslie Street Spit,* Friends of the Spit and Botany Conservation Group, 1992.

Hiss, Tony. *The Experience of Place.* Alfred A. Knopf, 1990.

Hough, Michael, *City Form and Natural Process: Towards a New Urban Vernacular.* Routledge, 1989.

Royal Commission on the Future of the Toronto Waterfront. *Regeneration: Toronto's Waterfront and the Sustainable City: Final Report.* Queen's Printer of Ontario, 1992.

Task Force to Bring Back the Don. *Bringing Back the Don.* City of Toronto, 1991.

Toronto Field Naturalists. *Toronto the Green.* Toronto Field Naturalists, 1976.

Varga, Steve. *Toronto Islands: Plant Communities and Noteworthy Species.* Toronto Field Naturalists, 1987.

Trail Organizations in the Greater Toronto Area:

Bruce Trail Association, P.O. Box 857, Hamilton, Ont. L8N 3N9

Citizens for a Lakeshore Greenway, P.O. Box 1067, Stn. Q, Toronto, Ont. M4P 2P2

Citizens for the Oak Ridges Trail, P.O. Box 28544, Aurora, Ont. L4G 6S6

Hike Ontario, 1185 Eglinton Ave. E., #411, North York, Ont. M3C 3C6

Metropolitan Toronto and Region Conservation Authority, 5 Shoreham Dr., Downsview, Ont. M3N 1S4

Brad Cundiff is a writer living in Toronto. He has a special interest in environmental issues, and his writings on the subject have appeared in a number of Canadian magazines.

Laura Klager has served as editor of Hike Ontario's newsletter, *Outlook,* and she is currently the editor of the Peninsula Bruce Trail Club's newsletter, *The Rattler.* Laura is an avid amateur naturalist and also secretary of the Waterloo-Wellington chapter of the Canadian Wildflower Society.

Evert Hilkers began his career as a graphic artist in Europe after the Second World War. After moving to Toronto in the early 1950s, he worked for some of Canada's largest advertising agencies and an art studio before forming his own successful graphic-arts company. Over the last decade, he has concentrated on fine arts, emphasizing painting as well as sketching.